TIME BEYOND TIME

Time Beyond Time

A Magical Memoir of Rural England

Hope Tod

With Illustrations by
Jill Barker and J. Ethan Brent

Sun on Earth™ Books

Heathsville, Virginia

Published by Sun on Earth Books

www.sunonearth.com

Illustrations: On pages 93, 125, 139 copyright by Jill Barker; on pages 17, 31, 38, 69, 105, 135, 143 copyright by J. Ethan Brent; and on pages 7 and 39 copyright by JupiterImages Corporation. Photograph on page xvi copyright by David Timperley.

Publisher's Cataloging-in-Publication Data

Tod, Hope

Time Beyond Time: A Magical Memoir of

Rural England/ Hope Tod. — 1st ed.

p.   cm.

1. Memoir—1940s.   2. England—Rural.

3. Sussex—Travel.   I. Title.

CT788.E54T63 2005

914'.2—dc21   PCN: 2005928177

ISBN-13: 978-1-883378-92-9

ISBN-10: 1-883378-92-3

Where blooms the never-withering rose,
And shines undimmed the immortal sun.
New joys and gems his beams disclose.
Time makes no stir, nor seasons run.

— From Time Beyond Time
by Gerald Bullett (1895-1958)

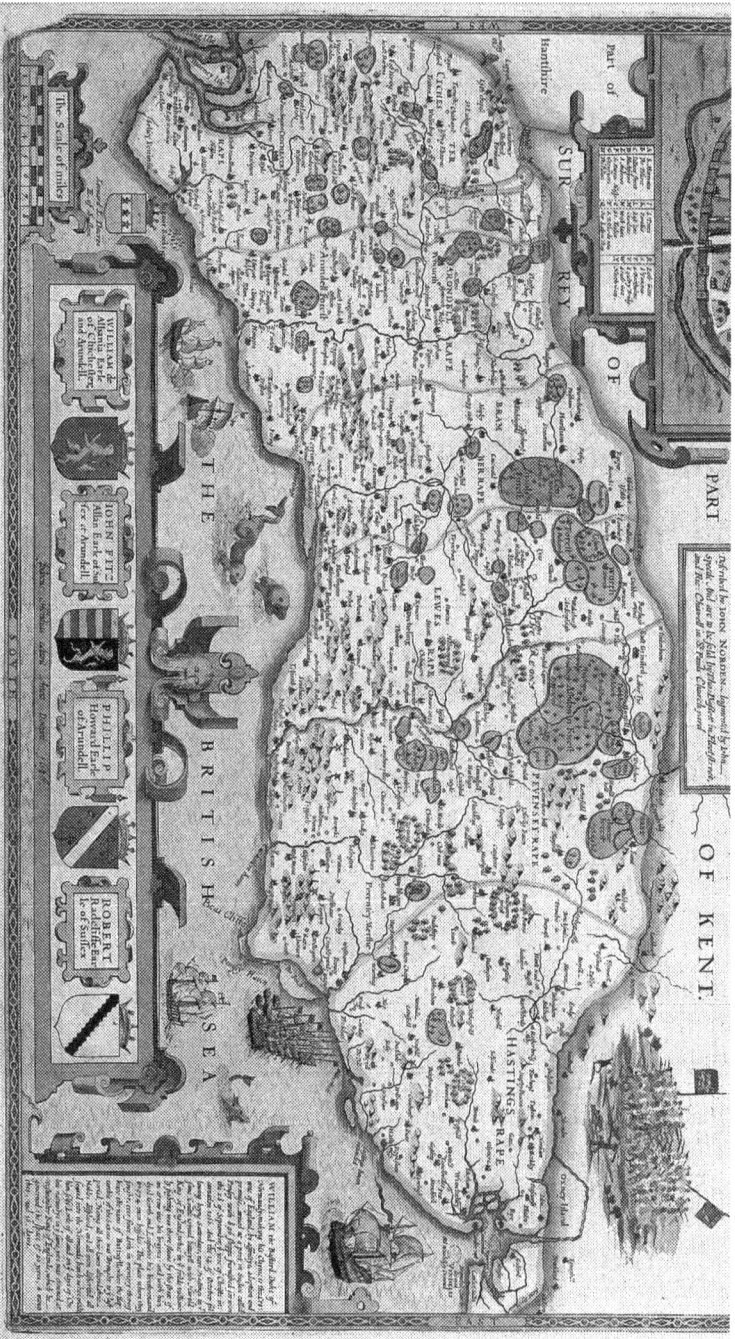

Hantshire

Part of

SUR

RY

OF

PART

OF KENT.

THE

BRITISH

SEA

WILLIAM de Albania Earle of Chichester and Arundell.

JOHN FITZ Allin Earle of Sussex & Arundell.

PHILIP Howard Earle of Arundell.

ROBERT Ratcliffe Earle of Sussex.

Described by JOHN NORDEN, Augmented by John Speede, and are to be fold by John Sudbury and Georg Humble in Popes head alley and Iohn Churchill in St. Pauls Church yard.

LEWES RAPE

BRAMBER RAPE

ARUNDELL RAPE

CHICHESTER RAPE

PEVENSEY RAPE

HASTINGS RAPE

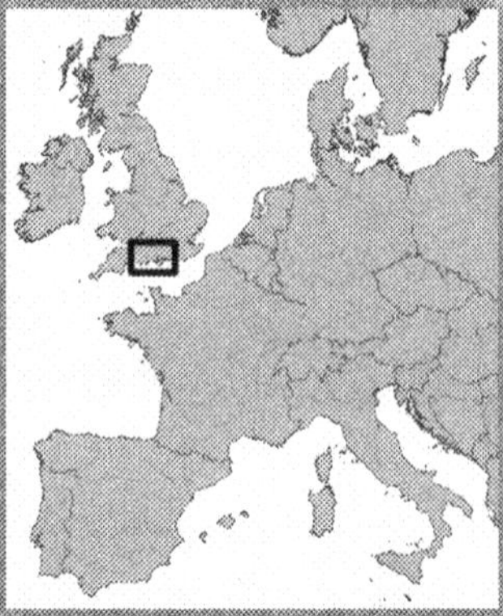

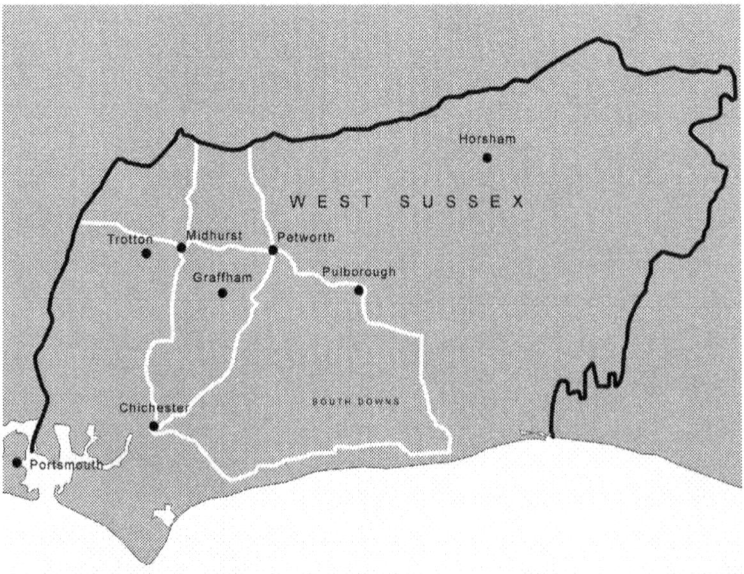
Horsham
WEST SUSSEX
Trotton
Midhurst
Petworth
Graffham
Pulborough
Chichester
SOUTH DOWNS
Portsmouth

The book you hold in your hands is the fulfilment of two solemn promises: the author's, Hope Tod, to her beloved husband, Dudley, shortly before his death from Parkinson's disease, that she would somehow complete her manuscript before they were reunited; and my own pledge, to Hope, as a fellow writer, to see to it that her latest book was indeed completed, if for any reason she could not do so herself. Hope, my dear friend, we've kept those promises.

The persons, events and circumstances depicted in this magical memoir recount a true life story—simple yet touching in its gentle pastoral simplicity—recollected from the author's loving memory of events more than fifty years earlier. Hope tells it with clear narrative skill and a remarkable tenderness of vision. Although the historical context of Hope's story is clearly set during and immediately after World War II (explaining her volunteer service in the Women's Land Army of Great Britain), she purposely makes scant mention of the war, reasoning in her gently insistent way that since so much has already been written about it, she would focus rather on the timeless qualities instead, which transpire more like those of a fairytale, in a time beyond time. Accordingly, some of the hard facts may well be selectively tempered and tenderly mellowed under the enchanting spell of her fond memory.

To me, as an anglophile American, Hope was superbly English. Born Marguerite Irene Hope Fawkes into a genteel upper middle-class family on 9 February 1917, she was the youngest of three

children. Her father was a respected doctor of medicine and a sur-
geon in the Royal Navy; her mother, the musically-talented daughter of a distinguished career diplomat, was a serene, tolerant and
gentle woman who delighted in gardening and growing ornamental
plants at their Sussex country house, sharing equally in her husband's love of ships and sailing on frequent family holidays, exploring the south coast in their sailing yacht, *The Kiwi.*

Looking back on her early childhood, Hope described it as a
simple and idyllic time, linked closely with the natural world, the
period when she was imbued with her parents' sterling qualities of
compassion and detachment. As a student at Bedales, the pioneering
co-educational boarding school in Hampshire (established on lands
given in part by her maternal grandfather), she thrived in its liberal
atmosphere full of eager vitality, enterprise, and originality, which
greatly sharpened her awareness, teaching her the importance of
listening carefully and observing distinctive shapes and forms, so
central to her thinking throughout her long life.

In addition to academic studies, her duties there included help-
ing in the school's gardens and on its farm (in keeping with her
great love of being outdoors, close to the earth). She learned the
useful, practical skills that would serve her later, such as hand-
milking cows, making butter, digging trenches, turning and carrying
hay, and hoeing vegetables. Her love of the patterns and textures of
nature found application in the weaving studio at Bedales, where
she worked with looms weaving intricately-designed fabrics that
she then crafted into 'wearable works of art'—smocks she kept her
whole life. I often admired them displayed on hangers hung on wall
hooks along the upper corridor under the massive rafters in Gauth
House, the enchanted Somerset longhouse she called home for more

than thirty years. Her interest in fabric design led to further training at the School of Arts & Crafts in Frankfurt, prior to the war, until the mounting political tension in Germany compelled her to leave. She continued her studies at an art academy in Paris, and then in London at the Central School of Arts & Crafts in Southampton Row, where she concentrated in the course on textile design.

It was around this time she met two men who were to become key figures in her life: at Cambridge, Dudley Tod, one of her brother's closest friends, the extremely tall lowland Scot with an appalling stammer whom she would marry in 1945; and Gerald Bullett, the well-known poet, essayist, and novelist, who lived not far from her family's Sussex residence. Although Bullett was twenty years her senior, he and Hope recognized one another as 'kindred spirits,' their mutual grasp of metaphysics and love for the natural world drawing them together in friendship for life and beyond.

Over the years, Hope and I grew very close—'family by choice'—neither of us having any immediate kin still living. Hope had given me so much support, for which I was eternally grateful, including the sage wisdom, comfort, and patient understanding I needed in overcoming the devastating blow of my best friend's death. 'Know that you always have a bolthole here, my dear,' she reminded me during our frequent transatlantic phone conversations. In 2002, I accepted her gracious invitation to stay four months as her house guest so I could begin chronicling (at Hope's urging) my account of this intense, complex friendship, for my own peace of mind. She always put great stock in the power of the written word, counselling me with, 'It's our legacy for those who come after us, you see.'

I returned to Gauth House a year later to help her complete the manuscript for this, her latest book. At 87, Hope's balance was not as steady as it had been in recent years, resulting in periodic falls. After each debilitating fall, she suffered health setbacks which took their toll. Her mobility became more and more restricted, until she spent most of each day stationary in her favourite oak Windsor chair at the kitchen table next to a large window. She seemed to have taken this limiting infirmity in stride. But a far greater loss for her as an avid reader was the dimming of her eyesight. It had deteriorated to the extent where she was no longer able to read, meaning it was impossible for her to make the necessary revisions to her handwritten manuscript on her own. (Consequently, I had sent her a mini-cassette recorder so we could exchange audio letters, to make our correspondence easier for her.) Adding to this frustration, Hope had been unable to find anyone locally even to type the manuscript up for her so that it could be submitted to potential publishers. Seeing that the odds were against her work ever becoming a book otherwise—as well as a perfect opportunity to give back a measure of the loving support I had received from her over the years—I gladly offered to come over and help her. Much to my delight, Hope embraced my offer with her customary graciousness.

Upon my arrival, I discovered, much to my dismay, this gracious lady actually needed far more personal care than her dignity and need for self-sufficiency allowed her to recognise or admit. I had come, as a devoted friend and fellow author, to help her keep her promise to Dudley. After that, I intended to travel on to a secluded seaside cottage in Donegal, Northern Ireland, to continue with a writing project of my own. But the six weeks I initially estimated for us to complete her book eventually turned into six full months. It was not our work on the manuscript that took so much time, even though I had to read it aloud for Hope, paragraph by paragraph, and then line by line, revising what she had already written and adding in new material as needed, typing it up as we went along, using the portable word processor I brought with me, a little at a time, each day.

Once we established this daily pattern for our collaboration, we were able to make fairly good progress. Hope's reminiscences on the period in her life covered by the book prompted us eventually to rummage about in desk drawers, cupboards and chests, ferreting out a whole cache of wonderful black and white photographs from those days (some of which are part of this book), old letters and relevant newspaper clippings, livestock listings and awards. Delving into the cavernous recesses of the dusty inglenook in the low-ceilinged, cobweb-festooned murkiness of the original slate-floored kitchen, with its huge open hearth and built-in bake ovens (vestiges from bygones days, centuries back, when the place housed a small band of monks), located just across the slype, we even got around to unearthing items salted away in the very steamer trunks Hope and Dudley shipped back with them on their return passage from India, half a century earlier.

What really took so much time to accomplish was setting up the necessary care for Hope. Up to that time, her neighbour had offered her kind, daily assistance. But I felt I could not leave until Hope's immediate future was secure: a simple goal in theory, but as I was to find out, quite challenging and very time-consuming to implement. The most daunting thing for me, as an American, was interacting with the various agents from the local, overburdened, bureaucratic government in making all the necessary arrangements for the entire range of daily assistance and support Hope needed in order to continue living in her own home for the rest of her life: such as someone to unlock the street door each morning and secure it again in the evening; to help her get up and dressed; to prepare her customary breakfast of biscuits and coffee; to feed her two beloved black and white farm cats, Piewacket and his daughter, Dandelion; someone to check and refill the coal-fired Aga stove twice daily so Hope would have heat, a stove for cooking and hot water; a laundry service that would pick up and deliver alternate weeks; a means to provide her with at least one hot meal a day on weekends to supplement a regular weekday lunch-delivery service; visits from healthcare professionals, the hairdresser every other week, the chiropodist every six weeks, etc. In setting up all of these arrangements, disruptions to Hope's familiar daily patterns were unavoidable, changes she understandably resisted, as 'an ancient light' of eighty-seven. While Hope had vivid recall for the smallest details of her life more than fifty years earlier, I grew concerned in noticing that her short-term memory was rapidly becoming less and less reliable. All this put stress on our relationship as close friends, living under the same roof. Sadly, when I bid her farewell—not knowing then it was to be for the very last time—beneath the outward assurances of reconciliation between us, there was still a palpable hint of tension.

Hope's life ended—in January, 2004—before her dream of finishing this book could be realised; yet, knowing her heart as well as I do, she would surely want for me to acknowledge in her stead the significant contributions of those special people who helped to make it possible.

Thus, I would like to thank her stalwart friend and attentive neighbour across the lane, the inspired poet Denise Crabtree Broom and her capable consort, Steve, for all their patient assistance which enabled Hope to live an independent life as long as she did; her two godchildren, Vanessa Mitchell and Richard Fawkes, for staying in touch and rallying around Hope in her time of need; all the kindness of her friends, neighbours and the caring constellation of local merchants in the community who provided her with vital services over the years as links to the wider world; my friend and soul sister, Jill Barker of Evercreech, master wood engraver, who made the journey to Gauth House expressly to meet Hope, showing her the tools of her craft while demonstrating the rudiments of their use, thank you for contributing some of your 'bespoken' creations which complement the beauty of her story so well; and to Hope's frequent visitors, Jonathan Stocks and Andy Andrews, for their many thoughtful gifts and fragrant bouquets, and all those otherwise lonesome days brightened by the charm of their youthful attention and the pleasure of whiling away the hours in good company over tea and biscuits, reading or simply chatting together in the study, close to the cosy fire. Bless you especially, Andy, for seeing our Hope through all the difficulties of her final days on earth. And all of you whom I have failed to commend properly, rest assured, gentle Hope is smiling upon you with her deepest appreciation, eternally.

Dudley, Hope's 'Bun' and true love, unquestionably, this loving memoir is dedicated to you, for your life-long devotion. Without the abiding inspiration of the pact between the two of you, she probably would not have got as far along as she did.

Finally, it would be remiss of me not to issue a heartfelt thanks to my true friend and tireless editor, A. R. Eguiguren, for his patient and insightful revisions in shepherding this project through to its culmination.

J. Ethan Brent

Lancaster County, Virginia, USA, June 2005

Hope Tod at her kitchen table in 2003

The Gypsy Caravan

Hope Tod at work in the 1940s with the Women's Land Army

In the days when dairy farmers still had their cows milked by hand, I worked as an Emergency Relief Milker for a large number of small dairy farms scattered among the Downs—an enchanted land in the rural heart of Southern England.

The Emergency Relief programme was part of the Women's Land Army, which provided a mobile labour force of women volunteers to fill the void left by nearly 50,000 farm workers recruited to fight World War Two.

The down lands' winding roads meander secretly through deep hollows which suddenly and quite unexpectedly emerge onto open fields. My working area was in West Sussex, between Petworth and Petersfield, where the open, high ground reveals a distant view of smooth, undulating, grey-green hills. The hills are crisscrossed by ancient, long-forgotten grass tracks that roam over and around the region, ending as mysteriously as they begin.

Slow-moving rivers flow gently beside lowland meadows, old farmhouses, and huge barns. These rivers curve gracefully through tiny hamlets and small villages, creating a spell of timelessness, of hidden wonders, and unknown things. The sun, the moon, and the stars play their lights across them, and the wind blows through in great and fast-moving squalls, scattering raindrops and snowflakes. There are always new delights to discover beside old humpbacked bridges and thrumming water mills. It's an ancient land that guards its secrets.

My work as an Emergency Relief Milker usually involved staying at a farmhouse or in a cottage when an accident (or sudden illness) befell the regular milker. These quite unpredictable emergencies needed the immediate help of someone able to milk the cows, feed the calves and other young stock, and generally attend to their needs, until the safe return of their regular cowman, or until a suitable replacement arrived. While it was challenging, hard work, I had been well trained for it. I could milk by hand and machine, understand the different aspects of stock rearing—with a sharp eye for details, a good memory, the ability to improvise, and my native quick wit, tempered by a diplomatic tongue!

Upon arrival on a given farm, I had to carefully study the animals put into my care. It was never an easy task, for I was a stranger to them. And yet, to watch the cows settling down so contentedly after the evening milking was a very satisfying ending to an often difficult first day.

My own accommodation in farmhouse or cottage was not always so comfortable. Gradually, it came about, as I moved from farm to farm, never knowing where I was to lay my head, that I became convinced it would be to my advantage if I emulated the snail and found a moveable home to live in. What I visualized and longed for most of all, was to find a traveller's wagon, just like those I had seen roaming the countryside during my childhood. The more I contemplated this snail-like existence, the more it fascinated me.

One summer evening, when the milking and the feeding of the calves was done and the dairy washed clean, I decided to take a ride on my bicycle in the hope of seeing or hearing about a caravan for sale. The evening air was cool and fresh after the heat of the milking sheds.

As I cycled slowly along the quiet lane, enjoying the shade from the high, leafy hedges, I breathed in the delicious scents which arose from the wide ditches, filled with meadowsweet and water mint. Soft sunlight dappled the surface of the roadway, shafting through the tall branches of the trees growing along either side. It was an enchanting evening, and I felt at peace with the world as I travelled along, visualizing my fairytale farmhouse on wheels.

Presently, some old cottages came into view. They were set back from the road and surrounded by low hedges. As I came close to them, I happened to glance over one of the hedges and thought I saw a traveller's caravan! I almost pitched myself over the handlebars when I applied the brakes to look again. And, yes, there *was* a traveller's caravan, exactly as I had visualised it: a gypsy caravan, traditionally built, brightly coloured, and standing on four large wooden wheels. It was an indescribable moment. I stood there gazing at it, spellbound.

As I looked more closely, I saw that it stood on a former vegetable garden which had access to the lane by a firm dirt track. I knew that I had to make contact with the owner, come what may.

I propped my bicycle against the hedge, opened the garden gate to the cottage, and walked up to the front door to knock. The door opened cautiously, and I met the questioning gaze of a middle-aged woman. 'Yes, what is it?' she asked me, still holding onto the door handle and looking at me rather anxiously.

'I have come to enquire about the caravan,' I replied, eager to make my request known to her. 'I would like to buy it, if it is for sale. And if it is, I was wondering what would be the asking price.'

She asked me to come in, and as I followed her along a passage, which led into a large living room, I told her my name and where I was working.

To my surprise, she did not seem taken aback by my request. Settling back into a chair, she told me that she and her husband, who was a publisher in London, had been seriously thinking of selling the caravan. They had originally bought it as an extra playroom for their two children. Although it had been very useful, the children were now adults and no longer needed it. She had no use for it either, and her husband complained that it took up too much of the garden, so they both would be glad to see it go to a good home. With the most delicious chuckle of laughter, which resonated around the room like an enchanted whisper, she told me the asking price. I was delighted and relieved that I could afford it.

Everything was happening so quickly, like a vivid, fast-moving dream. 'Can we go outside and look at it?' I said.

When we reached the garden and saw the van close to, and then carefully climbed the curved steps and entered, I knew that I had found exactly what I was looking for.

The inside was empty, except for two beautifully handcrafted, built-in cupboards. I stood, transfixed, imagining how I might furnish it and turn it into a travelling home in which I could live peacefully and independently, as I moved from farm to farm.

Immediately to the left of the entrance was the full-length hanging cupboard. Next to this was a compact little chest of drawers with an enamel top. The light from the window just above made it a good working surface for preparing food. Next was a small folding table which went flat for travelling or to make more space inside the van. Above the table was another little window.

6'3"

BOOKSHELF

FOLDING DOUBLE
BUNK BED

WINDOW

FOLDING
TABLE

COAL
RANGE

WINDOW

CHEST OF
DRAWERS

WINDOW

DINING
TABLE

10'

WINDOW

FULL-LENGTH
HANGING
CUPBOARD

ENTRANCE

CORNER
CUPBOARD

At the back of the caravan, the full width was taken up by the sleeping area, only six feet three inches across.

On the right was another table, with two folding chairs, one on either side. Finally, there was the corner cupboard—a complement to the hanging cupboard on the opposite side. The top half was for glasses, crockery, and food; the lower half was fitted out to hold water jugs and saucepans, so they wouldn't tumble about when the van was in motion. In between the top and bottom halves of this cupboard was a long drawer, to store cutlery. All was beautifully proportioned. Its doors were finished around their edges with a double layer of beading, small ornamental brass knobs, and a brass drawer handle of delicate design which completed the effect of a really charming, Georgian-style, corner cupboard—fit to grace the most elegant parlour. It was the prettiest internal fitting to any caravan I'd ever seen, and was a constant joy to gaze upon (as well as being most practical and roomy inside). The final refinement was the raised 'molly croft' roof, with its two, long narrow windows and two ventilators, which could be adjusted to eliminate cooking smells or to give just the right amount of fresh air.

'Well, what do you think?' the woman said. 'Do you like it?' I turned, looked her straight in the eyes and said, 'It's perfect. I will pay the full asking price and give you a cash deposit now and bring you my cheque for the remainder when I come to collect the caravan tomorrow. Will that be all right for you?'

Her face lit up into a brilliant smile, eyes sparkling with pleasure. 'Oh, yes, that will suit us very well indeed.'

We both laughed happily with relief, even though I had no idea at the time how I was going to get the van from the cottage to the farm. 'Come,' she said, 'let's go back to the living room. We will seal our financial transaction with a well-earned glass of sherry.'

In her living room, she brought out two glasses and a bottle of sherry. 'I am so glad you have bought the caravan,' she said. 'I know you will be happy living in it.'

I was touched by her awareness, and quickly assured her that I would take good care of it. We were both still rather breathless with excitement at the speed in which it had all come about. It was perfect timing. We had both been rewarded according to our individual needs.

With a warm handshake and my thanks to a kind, perceptive hostess, I walked down the garden path, closed the gate behind me, and dreamily started pushing my bicycle along instead of mounting it. I needed to be quiet within myself before starting back to the farm, entranced as I was with my accomplishment in purchasing my 'snail shell,' and the new life it offered to me. I must have walked quite a distance, in a dream-like state, when I became conscious that the air around me had become transformed by a brilliant golden sunset. Everything, as far as the eye could see, shimmered and glowed in this glorious light. I could feel its energy surrounding me. Was this a good omen, I wondered, as I stood still, absorbed into the shimmering brilliance?

Gradually, the numinous radiance started to fade and the colours dimmed. It was time for me to return to the farm, have supper, and get into my bed. Early morning milking beckoned. However, on my arrival and before going to bed, I decided to tell the farmer and his wife, who were in their living room, my good news: that I had just purchased a real gypsy caravan from the publisher and his wife who lived in a nearby hamlet, and that I planned to live in it, as soon as possible! Their gasps of surprise and amazement filled the room.

When the excitement subsided, the kindly farmer, to my delight, offered me the use of one of his shire horses, and the necessary tack to enable me to collect the caravan the following day. His wife also seemed pleased, perhaps knowing that she would be free of the responsibility of housing and feeding me during the remainder of my stay.

When I was safely in bed, the full helter-skelter of the day's events almost overwhelmed me, until I realized that tomorrow I might actually be living independently, in my own travelling home—always knowing where I would lay my head to sleep, always certain I had my familiar belongings around me, wherever I went. We would all travel along together! It was a deliciously comforting thought, which lulled me into dreamless sleep.

As soon as the morning milking was completed, the cows put in the paddock, the calves fed, the dairy washed clean, and the milking sheds swept out and tidied, the farmer came out of the house looking for me. He suggested placing the caravan close to one of his big buildings, conveniently near a water tap. This location would also give me shelter from the prevailing wind, and it was well clear of the cowsheds and the stable. The farmer had obviously worked it all out very carefully before suggesting it to me.

We moved on to the stable, where he prepared his old friend and favourite shire horse, Punch, a massive yet gentle animal. As I watched closely, the farmer set about harnessing Punch with the correct tack to draw the caravan. He warned me that Punch might be startled, at first sight, by the height of the caravan. 'Best to allow him a good long look and stand close to his head as you carefully back him into the shaves. Always stand close to his head and talk gently to him. He will then understand and not feel nervous. Be very close to his head and encourage him until the wheels of the caravan start to roll. It's all a matter of true harmony and reassurance,' he said.

Although I had often worked with shire horses and carts, I had no experience with a horse pulling a caravan. With Punch standing by my side, I felt confident and sure. I took his head, short rein held firmly in my right hand, and said, 'Come, Punch. *We* are going on an adventure.' Then, with a final small wave of my left hand to the farmer, Punch and I set off down the lane.

As we walked along the narrow lane, I talked softly to Punch, telling him where we were going and what we had to bring back to the farm; how high the caravan would be and how heavy I thought I was. When we arrived at the cottage, the kind lady came down the garden path to meet us and walk with us along the dirt track. She had placed the steps at the back of the caravan, and locked the door for safe travelling. I allowed Punch to have a good long look at the caravan before backing him gently between the shaves, all the time talking quietly to him, reassuring him that all was well. He stood with great dignity, and completely still, as the lady and I slowly raised the shaves, passing the chain across his back, then linking the caravan with his harness. I checked that his girth strap was firm and would not slip as he started to pull. Then, I quickly returned to his head and held the rein close to his mouth. Gently, I urged him forward. He gathered his strength as the caravan wheels started to roll. Punch quivered, then put his full strength into pulling. We were on the move! I stayed close to his head, talking quietly, whilst I steered him in the right direction. Slowly, the horse and caravan moved along the dirt track and onto the lane, where we halted, momentarily, to thank the kind lady for her help. 'Happy to do so,' she replied with a grin, looking longingly at Punch and the caravan. 'What a lovely sight they make! Have a safe journey back.'

With these reassuring words, combined with the bright sunlight of the summer morning, we started on the homeward journey.

Walking close beside Punch, my hand firmly on his rein and listening to the steady pace of his great big hooves pounding the lane, pure happiness filled my heart. How fortunate I was! The farm work was hard, I knew. But the rewards were wonderful—being able to do the work I wanted, with the animals I respected for their willingness to co-operate. As we plodded along, I became aware that Punch was as excited as I was by the prize which we were bringing into the farmyard together, to be placed carefully beside the big building. The farmer and his wife had heard our coming, and stood outside the house watching, fascinated by Punch's skill and determination.

Unhitching Punch from the caravan, I led him to the water trough for a well-earned drink. The farmer came over, smiling broadly, and said, 'Well done, both of you!' I complimented him on Punch's steady skill in marching the caravan safely home. As I spoke these words, Punch lifted his head from the trough, shook it vigorously and whinnied loudly, causing the bit in his teeth and brass on his collar to jingle, producing a really triumphant sound that echoed around the yard. The farmer laughed delightedly, and then proudly led Punch off to the stable to unharness and give him a good rubdown (and, I suspected, a small bowl of the best oats—a reward both horse and master well understood).

The farmer's wife went back into the house, and I walked across the yard to see my new travelling home. I carefully slipped the steps down and placed them against the step board between the lowered shaves. Then, with ever-increasing trepidation, I went into the caravan, closing the door firmly behind me.

'Have I made the right decision?' I asked myself, closing my eyes, as I stood within the empty, sunlit gypsy caravan. A deep stillness slowly enfolded me as I waited patiently for the answer to be revealed. Very gradually, I began to feel great warmth and a sense of security upholding me, welcoming me, and rejoicing with me. Then I knew, with complete certainty, that I *had* made the right decision. Without hesitation and in a clear voice, I heard myself say, 'Thank you, all, for my new home. I am so happy to have found it. All will be well, from now on, I promise you.'

I then opened my eyes and joyfully looked around me. It *was* so right! I stayed a further few minutes, enjoying the sensation of being inside the empty van, watching how the sunlight played across the four side windows and the tiny one high up at the back of the van. I was fascinated at the endless games it played with my eyes. It held my imagination, until I remembered that I had farm work I was responsible for. So, firmly but reluctantly, I went down the steps and back to work, looking forward to living in the van and learning all about its many hidden ways of coping with the natural world and the elements.

Outfitting My
Home on Wheels

Name _Miss M. I. H. Fawkes_

No. _34516_

You are now a member of the Women's Land Army.

You are pledged to hold yourself available for service on the land for the period of the war.

You have promised to abide by the conditions of training and employment of the Women's Land Army ; its good name is in your hands.

You have made the home fields your battlefield. Your country relies on your loyalty and welcomes your help.

Signed _C. D. Lehman_

Honorary Director

Signed _J. Burrell_

Chairman
Committee

Date _3rd July, 1940_

I realise the national importance of the work which I have undertaken and I will serve well and faithfully.

Signed _Hope Fawkes._

Women's Land Army Pledge card

W hen our midday meal was over, I cycled down to the village shops to buy food and necessities for life in the van. First, I went to the ironmonger's, where I bought a small oil stove, two bottles of paraffin, some candles, and a box of matches. I also found two tin mugs and two tin plates. I looked along the shelves until I spied a small kettle and a metal teapot, then a large cardboard box full of second-hand knives, forks, spoons, and other small implements. I picked out what I needed, adding a saucepan, a frying pan, and a small jug to my collection. Finally, I saw a large, circular, wooden breadboard, complete with knife.

At the grocer's, I had another box filled with butter, cheese, eggs, cornflakes, bananas, tea, coffee, sugar, marmalade and a big jar of Marmite. After a short chat with the grocer's assistant, I carried the box out and placed it upright in my big front basket, leaving enough room for a large loaf of bread, which I planned to buy at the baker's next door.

As I moved from shop to shop, I sensed a little ripple of curiosity building up around me. And when I went into the baker's, he handed me the loaf and said, 'Have you got visitors up at the farm?'

'I don't think so. Just me, doing the emergency relief milking.'

He knew about the accident to the cowman, so he hesitated, and didn't say anything more. I slipped quickly out of the shop, tucked the loaf in the basket, and set off back to the farm.

Cycling slowly, carefully balancing all my various purchases, I started to wonder what the village would make of my home on wheels—a gypsy caravan! My guess was that the news about the caravan's arrival at the farm would soon get around, and when I next visited the shops for fresh supplies, many guarded questions would be asked, in an offhand sort of way, but with eye alight and eager for any information to share and compare with neighbours. Anything new or unusual was a prize worth having—something to tell the other locals with authority and the delicious knowledge that *they* knew something the others did not! I promised myself that I would not disappoint anyone. I quite liked the idea of watching their faces when I told them all about my four-wheeled home.

Back in the caravan, I stowed the groceries and everything else in the small corner cupboard, set up the oil stove, inserting the big wick, and filled the base with paraffin. The assorted cutlery I placed in the drawer of the corner cupboard. The big brown loaf sat comfortably on the circular wooden board, which had two ears of wheat carved into its outer rim. Between the ears of wheat, the word *Bread* was neatly inscribed. The long, slender stalks wove right round the board, to complete the design. It was very pretty. The knife, with its strong wooden handle, snuggled up close to the loaf: *The Staff of Life*. The design seemed symbolic of energy and movement. It blended in so well with the elaborate wooden structure of the caravan and its beautifully carved embellishments. It made such a decorative effect, transforming the practical necessities of daily life into a vision of wonder and delight.

For my bed, I filled two large seed bags from the barn with sweet-smelling hay, which seemed to amuse the farmer when I asked for his permission. When the bags were tight full and tied up,

I hoisted them into the caravan, laying them together on the floor against the back end. They proved to be extremely comfortable to sit on. As a bed, they were cosy and aromatic. With my winter coat as a blanket, they soon warmed up and gently lulled me to sleep. The rest of my clothing, the Wellington boots and assorted shoes, I put into the full-length cupboard on the left-hand side of the entrance door. When I first opened it, I was surprised by its capacity. I could step right inside, if I wished, and there was still room for another person to join me. The clothes rail, which ran the full length of this cupboard, could accommodate a great many garments. It had, of course, been carefully designed to carry the whole gypsy family's wardrobe. It was also a safe place for storing valuables—very important for the Gypsies' well being. The caravan was full of surprises.

Earlier, the farmer's wife had offered me the loan of a beautiful white-enamel bucket to carry water from the stand tap, and a similar deep bowl for general washing and cleaning. I was also given permission to use their garden privy—a very comfortable shed, shrouded in ivy, with a stout lock on the inside. The long box seat had been so often scrubbed and sandpapered, its wood was smooth and almost white. Along the top of the seat were three holes of different sizes, to suit the whole family from childhood to large old age. At the far end of the seat was a pile of paper and magazines for reading and essential use. The floor was made of bricks, carefully laid and frequently washed. A large bucket of silver sand, with an accompanying shovel, provided the country equivalent of a city pull plug. The window was well curtained with a material displaying fat pink roses, golden lilies, and blue forget-me-nots.

By tradition, a bush of fragrant rosemary or lavender was always planted by the privy door, for aromatic reasons. One's approach to this little house involved a careful ritual of either whistling loudly or humming a song, to forewarn any occupant of the approach of another person waiting to make use of its comfortable seats. This ritual was invariably the same at each and every farm I visited. It was a traditional country code of practice, which must have been in existence for centuries.

When finished with the evening milking on this eventful day, and after seeing to the other animals in my care, I went back to the cool, clean dairy and filled an old jam jar with water, then with a bouquet of wild flowers that grew in such wonderful profusion all along the high hedgerows around the cow pasture. I marvelled at their brilliant colours and strong scents as I wandered round the field. The grazing cows took no notice of me. All was beautiful and serene in the soft evening light, with the cows contentedly chewing their cuds: a typical country scene, so timeless in its infinite beauty. I was quite lost in wonder and joy. It seemed as if I had stepped back into a simpler age, when there was time to just stand and stare. Time beyond time.

Anticipating the happy prospect of spending the first night in my new home, I had visions of a candle-lit supper and a good night's rest on straw. At the farm's gate, I happened to look down at the ground and, to my surprise, I saw a large snail slowly moving. I watched, fascinated, as it travelled with great determination towards a leafy green supper and a safe haven for the night. I then realised, with a feeling of recognition, that I understood how the snail was feeling, as I turned *my* steps towards my own self-contained, mobile home.

Carefully carrying Nature's gift of wild flowers, I mounted the five steps of the caravan and went inside—closing the bottom half of the door behind me—to prepare my candle-lit supper, which tasted especially good as I lingered over it, recalling the day's events. How beautifully everything had blended together. I wondered how the kind lady was feeling—surely relieved by having sold the caravan so quickly at this magical period of the full moon, as, in fact, it was tonight.

By the time I was ready to slide into my hay-straw bed, bright moonlight flashed through the caravan. Shafts of brilliant white light pierced the windows and the slim glass panels of the molly croft roof, slanting their pure, polarised light across the floor, making patterns of incredible beauty. One brilliant beam slanted through the jam jar containing the wild flowers. It shimmered like crystal, and the petals of the flowers looked like jewels. Even the aluminium kettle was transformed into a shining silver object. The common teapot glowed and sparkled like a newly made bronze vessel.

Totally enchanted, I lay on the bed watching this spectacular display. Everything shimmered and sparkled, glowed and reflected, making endless patterns of brilliant light—dazzling my eyes with wonders from the cosmic world of lights: colours, shapes, and forms. It was pure magic. And then, as I watched, I drifted into dreamless sleep.

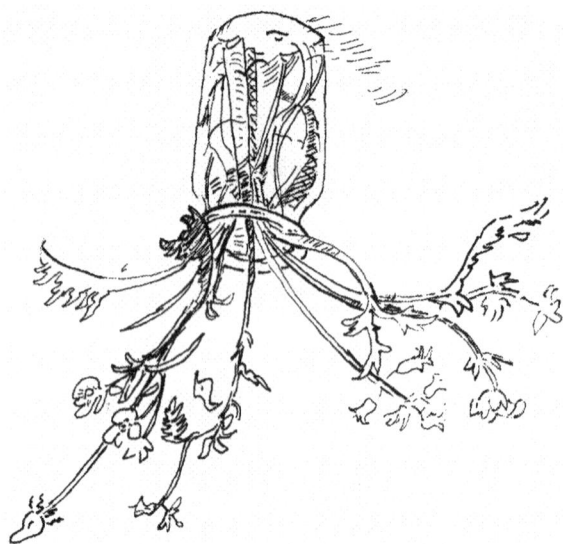

The Snail

Hope and her fairytale farmhouse on wheels

The pearly light of early morning and birdsong awakened me. At first, I did not know where I was. Then, my eyes took in the walls, the windows, and the various objects surrounding me. Of course, I was in the caravan! And this was the very first morning of my new life.

The sweet scent of meadow hay was all around me and the bed was deliciously warm. The light had awakened me a full hour and a half before my usual time. For a change, I decided to have my breakfast before going out to the morning milking, since I had the extra time. After washing and dressing, I lit the oil stove, which soon burned with a bright blue flame. The kettle, already half-full of water, I placed on the stove and waited to hear its boiling song. Whilst waiting, I fetched a knife, a plate, a mug, milk and sugar. I cut a thick slice of brown bread and covered it with a generous help-ing of butter and Marmite. I put tea in the pot and poured in the boiling water.

I would soon be able to furnish the caravan exactly as I liked, taking time to choose the right pieces for easy and comfortable trav-elling. So much to look forward to!

After tidying up the caravan and pulling on my Wellingtons, I opened the door and looked out. The sun was just rising, and the sky was a milky blue, suffused with pale yellow. It was going to be a lovely day. I moved quietly down the steps, closing the door firmly behind me. The yard was silent and still, but I could clearly hear the cows moving up to the gate of their pasture, snuffling along the hedgerow. I walked over to the milking sheds, where I put a small pook of hay into each manger, checking that all was ready in the dairy. Leaving the shed doors open, I halted for a moment. It was strange not to have come out of the farmhouse.

Eagerly, I walked towards the cow pasture, past the enclosed orchard, where I saw the cock with his hens, already occupied, calling to each other, giving the occasional chirp, and cackling as they found a particularly choice morsel buried among the orchard grasses and wild flowers. The beehives, also standing in the orchard beneath the fruit trees, were already humming away, the worker bees busily organising flights and waiting upon their queens.

When I reached the field gate, the cows were waiting for me. Before opening it, I looked down at the ground beside the gatepost, to see if my little friend, the brown snail, was anywhere about. I soon spotted its long silvery trail disappearing beneath a large stone, so I knew that it had survived the night and was not yet out and about. The snail must have been waiting instinctively for the vibration of the cows' hooves to pass by, before venturing out of its safe place under the stone.

After the milking, the cows were turned out into a fresh pasture, so there was no immediate danger for the snail. I couldn't resist running back to see if it had emerged from under the stone. It had, and was travelling along towards another green meal, quite determined to reach a large patch of mixed foliage. Again, I watched closely, amazed by the marvellous and mysterious structure of this tiny being. It looked so complicated, and yet, so very simple, and perfectly proportioned. The spiral shape of the shell was a miracle of efficient construction and design. No wonder that this mysterious creature should have been involved in myths and traditions for so many centuries—as a special and exotic food, particularly relished by the Romans, and also as a symbol of the spiral shape which has continually intrigued the human mind, and continues to do so to this day. Books have been written on the subject; learned men have pondered upon it with great insight and wisdom. I, too, felt a deep affection and admiration for this diminutive but important little creature, who had given me, through association, the idea of finding a home on wheels.

In the afternoon, I was busy with the young stock, letting the calves out into the small, enclosed pasture for exercise, where they enjoyed grazing on the short grass. They leapt around excitedly, playing in the sunshine. I watched them until they gradually settled down to serious grazing, and then my mind filled with ideas about painting the caravan—all of the beautifully carved wood of the canopy and its intricate undercarriage. I would have to visit the village ironmonger and choose suitable paints, brushes and sandpaper. I could paint in the evenings, after the final milking was done.

My mind was racing along, absorbed as I was with all the details. A small calf came over and stared at me, puzzled by the sight of someone standing stock-still in the middle of its meadow, and then it dashed off again to a new plot of grass, which did look so vividly green and lush. I continued to think of paint, brushes and sandpaper, and the decoration of my new home. Behind all of the practical thoughts was the constant delight in the realisation of how much the caravan would enrich my living. From now onwards, I was free to travel in the traditional way, carrying all my possessions with me, as the Gypsies had always done.

A Reading Van

Unidentified farmhand posing with the caravan

S oon after I purchased the caravan, a knowledgeable old friend came to have a look at it. I met him at the farm's gate, from where the caravan could not be seen, owing to the angle of the buildings. Welcoming my friend, I told him how glad I was to see him and to have the benefit of his extensive knowledge regarding gypsy caravans. As we walked slowly round the building, chatting, the caravan came into full view. My old friend halted, and then raised his right arm. Little gasps of delight escaped his lips. As we drew closer, I wondered what would happen next. He stopped right in front of the caravan, gazing at it with an intense expression. Finally, he turned to me, with his eyes shining, and said in an excited voice, 'Do you realise that you have actually bought a Reading Van? My goodness!' He explained that the Dunton family had started building them in 1874, in the town of Reading.[*] 'This is, indeed, a fine example of their craftsmanship,' he said.

'That's marvellous,' I said. 'Will you please go round and show me all that I do not know about it?'

He laughed good-naturedly, and slowly circled the van, pointing out the elaborate and beautifully carved undercarriage, with the

---

[*] Stylistically, Hope's caravan was actually a Burton type, most probably built by the renowned Dunton family of Reading, whose customers were primarily Romany folk. Broader and slightly taller than a typical Reading van, the Burton model has specific features, such as its distinctive shape, its measurements, the configuration of its under-carriage, the size and placement of its wheels, its flattened arch roofline with gutters and ventilating molly-croft skylight, the number of windows with shutters, and the characteristic weatherboards around its eaves, with the single porch brackets beneath them, fore and aft, but none on the footboard. Source: *The English Gypsy Caravan: Its Origins, Builders, Technology and Conservation*, by C. H. Ward-Jackson and Denis E. Harvey; Drake Publishers, Inc., New York, NY, 1973. pp. 145-147.

great, big leaf springs, which made travelling so comfortable. He then remarked on the massive wooden wheels with their copper hubs. 'You can always recognise a genuine Reading Van,' he said, 'by its careful construction and distinctive shape.' Next, he commented on the carved wooden decorations on the front and rear canopies, so ornate and flamboyant: big roses surrounding a mass of green foliage. 'Freshly painted, they would really look beautiful,' he added. At the back of the van, he showed me the pan box cupboard, for groceries and cooking utensils, plus the rack above it for carrying hay for the horse (of course) when travelling the road.

Continuing around, he told me that each Reading Van was unique, designed and built to meet the particular specifications of each individual owner, always with a singular motif. In the case of my van, the motif was the rose, which reached back in time to ancient Egypt—a fascinating thought. He pointed out the brake shoe hanging from its chain beside the rear left wheel, used for extra braking when going down steep hills. There was also another circular metal brake, worked from the front of the van by a small wheel that was close to the outside of the step board.

Upon examining this wheel brake more closely, he let out a cry of joy. 'Just look!' he said. And there it was—in neat white letters—on a tiny, black name board: *John Smith, Offham, Kent.*

'It's the name of the original owner,' he cried out with renewed excitement. I immediately picked up on this, saying, 'That accounts for the beautifully painted 'S' shapes on either side of the entrance door. Why, this is like a treasure hunt, so many new discoveries we've made, thanks to your great knowledge of old and unusual caravans. In this case, a genuine Reading Van!'

My old friend said all was in order and correct. In need of a fresh coat of paint, but otherwise, the van was perfect, even down to the little molly croft roof, with its slim ventilation panels on each side.

Inside the caravan, I offered him a cup of tea. Settling himself comfortably on my hay straw bags, he continued to look around him, at the cupboard, the windows, and the empty space. 'You have much to do to transform this into a real home,' he said. 'But, knowing you, I'm sure you will succeed brilliantly!'

I felt very happy and excited at this prospect, and promised him I'd do my best. But truthfully, looking after the various animals was my primary interest.

As he was leaving, he looked at me with the most loving smile. 'Remember, my dear,' he said, 'that living in a real gypsy caravan is a wonderful fairy tale. I wish you true joy and happiness in your new home.'

Working for Three Years

WOMEN'S LAND ARMY PROFICIENCY CERTIFICATE.

THIS IS TO CERTIFY THAT

Miss M. Fowles

W.L.A. No. 34516

HAS BEEN AWARDED A PROFICIENCY BADGE

IN *General Farm Work.*

Date *March 1944*

Signed *G. Denman.*

on behalf of the Women's Land Army.

Emergency Relief milking kept me busy and on the go, moving around my territory. I was constantly surprised by the variety of farms and the people who farmed them. In my travels, the van and I were always accepted, and my willingness to help out with any sort of extra seasonal work was understood and appreciated. It was work I loved doing, full of individual interest and unusual events.

Gradually, I collected many useful objects to furnish my home on wheels. My greatest prize was a small, three-cornered, cast-iron, coal-burning stove, which came to me in West Sussex. A blacksmith, hearing of my need, offered it for the very small sum of £3. He told me that he himself had no use for it, and was glad that it would be appreciated and regularly used. For me, it was an invaluable item of essential equipment. This little black stove was kidney-shaped, standing on four elegant legs with claw feet. It had a deep fire basket, with a wide ledge at the front, to hold the roasting dish. On top were two rings, which could be conveniently lifted off for feeding the fire or for a quick boil of the kettle. At both corners were small, decorative faces, like ancient church effigies. The whole of it was beautifully decorated with an ornamental edge, also in cast iron. It was the most intriguing little stove I had ever seen.

I asked a local carpenter to come work on the van so the stove could be used safely. First, he placed a sheet of fireproof material on the centre of the wall on the left-hand side of the van. Then, he put a similar piece on the floor, since the van was made entirely of wood. Next, he fitted a long chimney stack to the back of the stove, sealing it carefully.

'Lovely little stove, that,' he said when he completed his work. 'Good to see the smoke coming out of the chimney so well.'

Inside the van, it soon warmed up and became very cosy. I opened the little molly croft ventilators to allow fresh air to circulate. With my straw bed, a small chest of drawers alongside the big hanging cupboard, the coal-burning stove, a table on the opposite side with an oil lamp on it, two chairs, and curtains at the four windows and the top half of the door, it really was home! I felt sure that my knowledgeable old friend would approve of all my efforts. I just wished he were there, in person, to smile and say, 'Yes, I do like it, very much, indeed. I also like your paintings on the walls and your books on the end shelf. It's all so complete.'

When I talked with friends and told them what I was doing, they looked surprised that I should have chosen such unusual work—so different from my former way of life. 'But don't you find the twice-daily milking repetitive and boring?' one said. 'Such a tie to the cow's tail,' another one jokingly put it.

I replied that it was different each time. There was infinite variety with the cows. Each was a unique animal, and yet, a member of the herd. I had come to the amazing realisation that hand-milking a cow was a very rewarding occupation, requiring patience, trust, and the right approach.

The cow produced milk for the calf, so my hands had to replace the eager calf's mouth. Gentle but firm handling—milking her out quickly—always helped the most; whereas a rough, unyielding, angry word, or a loss of temper, could bring problems. The cow knew instinctively what should be done. If not done correctly, it kicked in a defiant way, and soon the bucket was tipped over! It all looked simple, but it was, in fact, a complex process, which, if done with real skill and patience, had its rewards.

Some cows, I found, had the most unusual tastes. For instance, a little black Kerry cow adored Fox's Glacier Mints. Before starting to milk her, I offered one to her on the palm of my open hand. A large, brown tongue swept it off into her mouth, and she trundled it happily, round and round her mouth, as I milked her, easily and quickly! It was a lovely little ritual between us, and it gave us both so much pleasure.

Another cow, an Ayrshire, dearly loved small apples, and munched them up with such relish. As an Emergency Relief Milker, I always tried out and discovered these little preferences. It helped to make the milk flow easily, at a time of disturbed routine, caused by the absence of the regular cowman. And it did bring a smile to the farmer's face, when he realised that the milk yield had gone up, in spite of a stranger milking his cows.

If my stay on a farm was a longish one, due to serious injury to the cowman, I had to establish a sound routine. This I did by always doing the same things in the same way. Cows are creatures of habit, and like to take their time. You can't rush them. Otherwise, they panic and tend to push and shove. So I observed them carefully and silently, for the first few days, noting each animal's reactions. Their sense of humour often surprised me, and their innate wisdom frequently startled me. It made me consider carefully before I acted on their behalf. Their progression from the pasture to the milking sheds had to be done correctly and in order of seniority. They had a very marked sense of priority on these occasions. Spring, summer, or autumn—the procession was always the same: I would walk ahead, and they would follow, sometimes lingering over a particularly lush clump of grass, and then hurrying to keep up with the others, and not lose their places in the orderly queue. They would enter the milking sheds knowing exactly where their own manger was—the place which always held their special titbits.

As they munched eagerly, I tied up their neck halters. Then they felt safe and waited their turn to be milked. I always began by grooming and then washing down the udder with warm water for hygiene. Each cow's teats were tested by drawing a few drops of milk into the little metal testing cup. If all was well, I would start milking, sitting on my three-legged stool, close to the cow, with my pail lightly held between my knees, pulling rhythmically at the back two teats and then the front pair. Often I would sing to the cows as I milked, which seemed to please them. Their favourite tune was a really lilting waltz, with a strong rhythm! As nobody else was around at milking time, I could sing to my heart's content, and, I hoped, for the cows' enjoyment.

Each farm that I visited as an Emergency Relief Milker was in a state of anxiety, so my first job upon arrival was to organise a routine, as far as possible, similar to what the particular cows were accustomed to—attend to and check the various young stock, and make myself familiar with the layout of the various buildings. Next, I would offer to help with the seasonal work, doing it between milkings. Some farms had more cows than others, but they were all small, mixed farms. A few had a resident bull, which ran with the herd. Some shared a bull with several neighbours. I was never quite sure what I would find, but I became used to adapting and coping with all the various circumstances.

In this way, I learned very many different and useful skills. Depending on the time of year, I would help with the hedging, ditching, mowing, lifting the root crops with horse and cart, and hay cutting from the stack. I loved the latter. The big knife, sharp and shiny, cut through the hay like a knife through butter. The scent of the fresh-cut hay was like expensive, mellow tobacco—fresh from the tin, sweet and pungent.

The pigsties were usually in the main yard, handy for feeding. I would go over and scratch the sow's back. How she relished this attention, standing still with eyes closed, wafting herself back centuries, to the days when pigs were semi-wild, living in the forest, feeding on the lush vegetation, scratching themselves on the low branches of the various trees. Several farms regularly collected the acorns in season, so they could be ground up to supplement the pig meal of barley. This interested me so much, as nothing was wasted which could be used for the benefit of the animals. The acorns gave the pigs a good, varied diet of natural foods. In the winter, a well-mixed meal of warm water, milk, barley, and ground acorns brought the pigs to the trough with squeals of sheer delight.

The poultry (or fowls, as some farmers called them) roamed the yard. In the daytime, they were free to meander into the nearby copse or small meadow close to the yard to seek worms, grit, and whatever else they could find to their liking. Towards evening, they loved to gather on the branches of the nearest tree and often had to be shooed down into the safety of their big wooden shed, which contained long perches, as well as straw-lined nesting boxes for the laying hens to use. All of them had to be safely locked in at night, against the ravages of the wily fox.

I was intrigued by some farmers calling their hens *fowl*. It was an ancient term, and part of their original name: jungle fowl. The birds had come originally from the Far East, and they were gradually domesticated. It was the forest that still attracted them, as it does so many other birds. No farmers I knew wanted to have guinea fowls on their land—in spite of their excellent, gamey flavour and the ease of feeding them—because they were impossible to catch and made so much shrill noise as they roosted in the trees, refusing utterly to come down at night. They were too wild to run with the chickens.

So many different animals, all sharing the big yard, gave us constant entertainment and, at times, unexpected surprises. Sometimes, the young pullets played at a game of 'who dares' with the shire horses, as the latter came into the yard after the day's work. The horses would halt, looking down from their great height at a cheeky little pullet, flitting close to their big hooves, tweaking their hairy fetlocks. Then, they would toss their heads until the brass on their harnesses jingled loudly. Slowly and with care, they would move into the sanctuary of the stable, leaving the silly little pullets to squeak and call out in shrill excitement at such a daring exploit with the huge horses. All was done with such eager excitement and daring that it made us laugh.

Many downland farms also kept a flock of sheep, which only came into the farm's big barns for lambing, to be safe from bad weather, badgers, otters, and foxes. A few farms built special, temporary lambing pens outside, made of many bales of straw covered over with cast-iron roofs and enclosed with fencing hurdles. Shepherds and dogs worked night and day during the lambing season. The rest of the year, the sheep (which were mostly Southdowns) lived on the downland, cropping the sweet, short turf, literally covered in wild thyme, that some say gives their meat such delicious flavour for the traditional Easter celebration of roast lamb and mint sauce with redcurrant jelly, accompanied by at least four different vegetables, their flavours blended with a rich gravy.

Life was homey and leisurely. There was time to appreciate the little hidden things, as well as the majestic beauty of the rolling downland as the four seasons of the farming year flowed along.

The van was deliciously warm in winter with the coal-burning stove. I had books to read and ponder over, and the endless delight of privacy! As I moved from farm to farm, the van and I travelled along together, complete in every detail. Each move involved the use of a shire horse for the journey, usually supplied by the farmer who was in need of urgent help.

For three years, I moved around from farm to farm, performing my Emergency Relief Milking craft, becoming very adept at siting the van in just the right place—sheltered between the buildings, close to a stand tap for water, and not too far from the traditional outdoor privy!

I learned a great deal of sound farming knowledge, and I was always careful not to intrude on the personal lives of the farmers and their wives. After all, I was an Emergency Relief Milker, come to help them at a difficult time—not a guest. Bringing my own home with me made life much easier for them, as well as for myself. During the three years of constant change, I learned to be quick, quiet, and to listen to the cows and any advice from the farmers, wherever I was. Life, in general, travelled at a steady pace.

Reunion and India

Hope and Dudley Tod in India, 1945

I received a cablegram from South India which read, COMING HOME ON LEAVE. PLEASE LET'S GET MARRIED. WILL YOU MARRY ME? Dudley, my truelove, was finally returning, after nine years' separation!

At long last, our dream was really coming true. I stood in the van, cable in my hand, transfixed by wonderful flights of imagination and ecstasy. In my mind, I called out, 'Yes, oh yes, please!' and I longed to feel his strong arms around me, warm and safe, at last.

After the evening milking, when all was complete, I returned to the van, recalling all that we had experienced together: our first chance meeting, in my brother's rooms at St. John's College, Cambridge, where my truelove called in to discuss something. They were friends and attended the same college. And I, too, just happened to be visiting my brother at the time, also with questions! Then followed lovely memories of parties, dances, and theatre outings in London, visits to art galleries, showrooms, and meals at the Savoy Hotel—our favourite meeting place. The memories flooded in, reminding me of the many adventures we had shared together, thus far, Dudley and I, and those yet to come—endlessly and for ever.

Would Dudley like the van? Would he understand how much I loved working on the land with the animals? Would he? Oh, yes, I was *certain* he would. The stove was still burning brightly as I snuggled into my hay bed, still remembering, still dreaming, and looking forward.

The next morning, I wasted no time in alerting the Women's Land Army, telling them my good news, and asking them if they could find another Emergency Relief Milker to take my place at the next farm. I told the farmer and his wife about the cable I had received, and assured them that I would complete the final two weeks with them, so that all would be in order for their cowman upon his return to work.

My next problem was the safe storage of the van. I telephoned around to farming friends who had large barns. To my surprise and relief, Alec Monro, a dear, old Highlander, whom I had often helped, offered to store the van in his vast old Sussex barn. It would be quite safe, he told me, in one of the big unused bays. I was grateful to Alec for his generous offer, and arranged to deliver the van when I had completed my current assignment. He quite understood, and seemed genuinely pleased to be of assistance. Alec knew the van well, and he often expressed his admiration for its beautiful carvings and bright colours. The van was my most precious possession, so I gave thanks for its safe storage and the careful attention I knew it would receive during our sojourn in India.

Our reunion took place in Dudley's godmother's beautiful old house in Chelsea. He was waiting for me in the drawing room, standing so tall and upright—all six-foot four of him. As I entered the room, I hesitated, overcome with excitement and trepidation after our nine-year separation. I saw that he was quivering with excitement. I, too, felt as if I would faint. For a long instant, we both stood gazing at one another. Then he moved quickly towards me and enfolded me in his arms. I felt his warmth, his strength, and his love. I was speechless with joy! It was the most *wonderful* moment

of all. We were together again, and all was well. The years of waiting evaporated in the glow of that marvellous moment.

We had an enchanting London wedding on 3 March 1945, surrounded by family, friends, and so many presents. There was warm
sunshine, and blue skies. Our honeymoon started at the Savoy Hotel—where else? We dined and visited the theatres in the evenings
and walked through the great parks by day, revelling in all the sights
and sounds, and the beauty of London town (to the starry eyes of a
newly-wed couple, at least).

We then went on to Cambridge, for two weeks of commemo-
rating the days of our first meeting. We took our bicycles, of course,
and rode over to Grantchester and to Hemingford Grey, and so
many other fondly remembered places. We also visited the Market
and made purchases in Heffer's Bookshop, ending up with a huge
meal in the Indian restaurant across the square.

Our sea journey to India completed our honeymoon in the
most delicious, romantic way: across the Mediterranean to Suez,
down the canal to Aden, and then across the Arabian Sea to Bombay [Mumbai]. Our destination was Madras [Chennai], in South
India.

When we landed in Bombay, the heat was extraordinary! We
planned to complete our journey by the Madras Mail train, a mon-
ster steam locomotive that roared right across the country, from
west to east. With the heat, the milling multitude, and the noise like
an explosion, the air-conditioned refuge of our two-seater compart-
ment was a godsend. Will I ever get used to the heat, I wondered?
The large, airy buildings—with their merciful ceiling fans and wide
verandas—did keep one cool, for the Madras heat was extremely

humid. When my blood finally thinned down, it would become more comfortable, I was told. I understood that this process took about six months, which seemed a long time to suffer!

Madras is a fascinating, ancient city. Its great harbour and long marina usually carried a breeze in the evenings. Dudley's office was on the First Line Beach, in a great white building which replaced an earlier one, built in 1788. Dudley was the manager of the shipping and transport department, which kept him very busy, organising, linking, and arranging the movement of all manner of materials and goods to every part of the world.

Our bungalow, which had originally been an Indian *zanana* (i.e., ladies' quarters), had a very long drive down to its secluded site on the banks of the Adyar River. The garden was quite large, surprisingly green, with many beautiful tamarind and banyan trees. There was also a vegetable garden, stocked with a type of bean called Ladies' Fingers, as well as tomatoes, radishes, and other typical plants. Bougainvilleas and trailing creepers roamed around the garden, creating colour and shade. The shrubs were varied and gloriously coloured. Our water supply came from a big Indian-style, open water tank which ran along the side of the bungalow, and was inhabited during the mating season by a multitude of frogs.

The long driveway terminated in a large semi-circle of gravel, backed by a wide border of big cannas, also planted in a semi-circle. This created a very colourful and lovely foil to the entrance of the house, with its deep veranda and yet more bougainvilleas. Madras in those days was so lush and green and spacious.

While Dudley worked long and hard in the vast European building down by the harbour, I was selected to be Secretary of the room of women's work, the Victoria Technical Institute, which turned out to be just a very large double-fronted shop on Mount Road, where fifty-two different missions of all denominations sold their wares. It was known as the V.T.I. and displayed and sold the most beautiful embroidered garments, children's clothing, luncheon tablemats, and so many other items.

In South India, our attempts to settle into a job with a large mercantile firm were not altogether happy. With independence for India looming, the situation there was becoming very unstable for foreigners, especially the British. I found the intense heat extremely trying. Life was so different and so strange. Dudley began to suffer badly from dengue fever combined with septic prickly heat, a painful condition caused by the oppressive heat and high humidity. We consulted two doctors on the situation, and both, with many years of service in the East, concurred in their diagnosis: 'Leave the tropics, as soon as possible.' We took their advice and decided to return to England.

Over the years, in the course of our correspondence during our nine-year separation—with me back in England and Dudley over in India—we had often discussed moving to the south of England to farm together. The idea grew and grew in my imagination, so that I began to long to be home again. Although we had enjoyed our travels around exotic India—on business as well as purely for pleasure, visiting so many new cities, ancient temples and shrines, a continent rather than a country, filled with millions upon millions of people— I longed for the cool Sussex Downs and Hampshire, the special quality of light and the seasons, and the incredible beauty of its lush, green landscape.

After carefully talking it through together, night after night, Dudley handed in his notice and booked our passage home. We then started to organise the packing up of our Indian residence, making certain that all eight domestics we employed had suitable new positions to go to. It had been an amazing experience living there, learning to know the people and their ways. I would always hold them in my heart, especially the servants with whom I shared our home. They were so loyal and willing to please.

We sailed from Bombay and had a leisurely and comfortable journey, travelling by ship because, by this time, we had accumulated quite a lot of possessions. During the voyage, we often sat on the deck far into the night discussing our plans for the future, and the various ways in which we could earn a living. Neither of us was attracted by the 'big money.' Rather, we wanted a congenial way of life in the country. So we decided to look for farm work. Our ultimate objective was to have a small dairy farm of our own. Never having done any practical farm work, Dudley thought the best way for him to learn was to work for other farmers. We finally settled upon hiring ourselves out to any dairy farmers, and to use the gypsy caravan as our mobile home.

Upon arrival in England, we saw once again green fields and flowering hedgerows, heard the song of the blackbird, and felt the soft rain on our faces. My heart sang with pure joy, and Dudley gave me the most radiant smile as he looked straight down at me and exclaimed, 'Home *and* the van. Wonderful! I can't wait to get started.'

I looked around us at the early summer morning, with its pale blue sky and gentle sunshine, and suddenly felt a warm little breeze fluttering gently around us, welcoming us home.

Back from India
and Restoration

Hope and the restored caravan

We travelled by train down to Sussex to the farm of our Highlander farmer friend, Alec Monro. The three of us approached his ancient, cavernous barn. With effort, he and Dudley opened one portion of the heavy doors and, together, we peered in the darkness inside. A single shaft of brilliant light pierced the gloom. It came from an open pitch hole (used to toss in the hay) three-quarters of the way up the wall at the far end of the building. Moving carefully, we entered. And, as our eyes grew accustomed to the dim light, we could make out the form of our gypsy caravan, resting in one of the far bays.

In the shelter of this glorious old building, with its sweeping roof timbers and great supporting pillars, and its protective and tranquil atmosphere, the little caravan looked completely at home. We stood together in silence and looked, lost in the wonder of it all. The perfection and beauty of disciplined craftsmanship had us all enthralled. Then, anxiety over the caravan's condition broke the spell. We drew closer to examine the wheels, undercarriage, and superstructure, for any signs of woodworm or decay. The paintwork, naturally, was badly chipped, and some of the felloes in the large wooden wheels would need attention. Otherwise, all seemed to be sound and in good order. I turned to Alec to thank him for his kindness in looking after the caravan whilst we were away.

'Ach, aye,' he said, 'It was a real pleasure, to be sure. And now, there she is: your own wee home, and on wheels, too—that's a grand thought!'

It was, indeed. No house hunting for us, and no long hours of housework for me! Dudley was also smiling gently, because he, too, understood how very much I loved the van. To find it safe and sound, after the years of separation, was quite wonderful.

While Alec busied himself in another area of the barn, Dudley and I discussed how we were going to move it to the wheelwright's yard in the village, about five miles away, where we planned to take the van for repairs, alterations and painting. As I examined the shaves, still neatly attached, I remarked, as Alec rejoined us, 'We will need a horse.'

With a sigh of resignation, Alec said, 'I'm afraid they're all gone, dearie. These past few years have completely changed the life of the cart horse, the draft horse and a great many ponies, as well. It's all changed now. We farmers have tractors these days.'

I was amazed and quite shocked by this revelation. And yet, as we returned home from Liverpool by train, I had noticed that there were many more tractors working the land than before. 'Is this post-war progress?' I asked Alec. 'Yes, I'm afraid it is, dearie—strange, but true. Why don't you have a drawbar fixed on your caravan, and Dudley can tow it to the wheelwright's yard with my tractor.'

It was not what I had expected, but that was what we had to do. As there was no alternative, Alec's forward-looking mind had simply accepted the change.

So we towed the van slowly and carefully to the wheel-wright's yard. I travelled inside, experiencing the strange, new sensation of being propelled along behind a tractor, instead of walking beside a horse. Although the change was sad at first, I soon became accustomed to it. The van itself was still the same. And to me, just as beautiful. Life is continual change, after all—for better, or for worse. Who was I to judge? We were heading in the right direction, anyway: to the wheelwright's yard.

Great care has to be taken when towing an old-fashioned caravan by tractor. The large wooden wheels, with their metal hoop tyres, tend to heat up quickly on the tarmac surface of modern roads. And the felloes, which shape the wheels, are apt to warp with the heat and fall out. Also, the height of the caravan has to be taken into consideration when travelling beneath the low-hanging branches of trees. And then, there was the chimney stack: it had a nasty habit of getting caught up in low limbs and loosing its cowl. So our progress was, of necessity, slow and cautious.

I leaned out of the door to watch out for low branches and shout to Dudley to take heed. We had some narrow misses, but my main difficulty was getting Dudley to drive slowly enough, since he'd never before driven a tractor, and the speed was hard to judge, there being no gauge or indicator. I was guided by the intensity of the vibration I felt inside the caravan. When it became too severe, I shouted, 'Whoa!' as loud as I could over the din of the tractor's engine. In acknowledgement, Dudley raised his hand and slackened the speed. This makeshift signalling system worked very well for us, and we arrived safely at the wheelwright's in the hamlet of Trotton, situated on high ground above the wide River Rother.

The wheelwright's yard was on flat ground, well clear of the road, with a wide sweep in front, allowing carts and wagons to draw in close to the workshops. Dudley drew the van up outside the carpenter's shop and switched off the tractor. Blissful silence! We heard the birds calling in the trees overhead around the shop. I descended the steps from the van and looked around. It was so peaceful and quiet. The hush of antiquity pervaded the whole area.

Presently, the carpenter emerged from his workshop looking with interest at the van, and then said he'd call the boss. Whilst waiting, we ventured into the carpenter's deep, mysterious domain. Long benches covered the entire length at the back, and wood shavings carpeted the floor. Over all was the clean scent of wood, freshly cut and laid out along the work benches. The windows, which ran along the front of the building, were dappled with cobwebs festooned in minute wood shavings, creating a striking effect as the sun shone brightly through them. The interior was a treasure trove of tools of every description. Paintbrushes were head up in empty jam jars. Paint pots were stacked on shelves. Files, saws, and screwdrivers, of all shapes and sizes, hung against the wall. On the overhead beams, there were long planks and sheets of hardboard. Every imaginable timber variety seemed to be stored above our heads. A pot of glue bubbled gently on a tiny fire alongside one of the benches, exuding its familiar smell. We were enchanted by all this display of craftsmanship. I breathed it in deeply as I watched Dudley leaning against the door of the workshop, quietly taking it all in.

Our reverie was suddenly interrupted by the sound of the carpenter's footsteps. 'He'll be out in a jiff,' he said, going back to his work. Presently, the boss emerged from his house, came over and greeted us in a businesslike fashion. He was a short, compact man with thinning hair, quick eyes, and exacting speech. He took a slow walk around the van, looking closely at the undercarriage and the wheels.

'She's in good condition, considering her age,' he said. 'Haven't seen one like this for many a year. Reading Vans, they called them. Used by the real gypsy folk. You can tell by all the beautiful carvings and ornamental painting of the woodwork, and this big carved turntable for the shafts, and these great leaf springs, for balance and comfort. Beautiful workmanship! Not many of these left nowadays. Must be all of eighty or ninety years old. These wheels need attention, and some of the superstructure could do with new battens. Now let's have a look inside, shall we?'

Because of its many small windows—two on each side and one at the back, higher up—plus the glazed upper half of the entrance door, the caravan was very light and gave the impression of size, despite the fact that it was only ten feet long, six feet and three inches wide, and six feet six inches high. This last measurement was of great importance to us both. Since Dudley's height was six foot four inches, he would have found life inside the van most difficult otherwise.

Dudley and the wheelwright were soon immersed in planning a new double bunk to be built across the end of the caravan, to replace my improvised bed. The new bunk bed was to be of the folding variety, so that in the daytime it formed a sofa seat. There would be two large storage cupboards beneath to hold the blankets, sheets, and pillows, with enough extra space for our shoes.

Whilst the men discussed technical details and made their many measurements, I sat on a seat and looked out one of the caravan's side windows. It was like peering through a magic casement, for framed within it, I saw the forge and the carpenter's workshop against a background of trees and fields and a tiny patch of brilliant blue sky. The colours seemed to vibrate. The impression was vivid in its clarity. I thought, Is this how the travelling folk saw life as it passed them by? This is what it must have felt like to live as a family in a house on wheels—the inside, always the same, blessedly familiar; the outside scenery continually changing. Was this why travelling folk were so often cheerful and light-hearted? Was this wonderful feeling of *security with mobility* an important, even vital, factor in their nomadic lives? I wondered how many other women had looked out of this very same window over the years—watching for a lover's return, keeping an eye on small children at play; or, perhaps, with fear, as the Law came along to tell them to move on.

The caravan rocked gently as the two men moved about. As it did, I experienced the sensation of being rocked in a cradle—that archetypal feeling of fundamental security and womb-like comfort, the perfect, contained balance for a travelling life.

As the wheelwright was already extra busy with various other promised jobs, and we were pressed for time and anxious to start living in the van, we suggested doing the repainting ourselves, just as soon as the new bunk bed was completed and the wheels and superstructure repaired. He readily agreed to this; and, with a firm handshake, he and Dudley sealed the deal. For our convenience, he said we could leave the caravan in his yard and do the painting there. And so, for the next few weeks, we became members of the workshop and joined in with the laughter, gossip, and many cups of tea brought out to us by the wheelwright's wife. It was a privilege to be accepted by these highly skilled craftsmen, and to enjoy the benefit of their interest and knowledge about the structure of our traditional gypsy *vardo* (as the English Gypsies called these wagons). The craftsmen were always ready with all sorts of useful information and advice about such things as paint and putty. And when we had at last finished the jobs, they were generous with their praise over our amateur craftsmanship and ability as painters and decorators.

When the smell of fresh paint inside the caravan finally cleared, and all was dry and firm, we started on the outfitting: curtains of striped, thick Indian cotton cloth we'd brought back with us, expressly for this purpose, to cover the small windows; crockery, glasses, suitable pots and pans, plus cutlery for the corner cupboard drawer; two large spring mattresses for the new bunk bed (which, when pulled out, made up into a large double bed, six feet by four feet. In the daytime, they converted easily into a sofa, with one to sit upon, the other serving as a backrest). We purchased a large, covered bin for rubbish, and the biggest bucket we could find at the ironmonger's for water. These would sit on both sides of the step board and save me running in and out many times a day. All I had to do was lean out of the door to dispose the rubbish on one side, and dip for water to make tea or for washing up on the other. The lid on the rubbish bin prevented marauding animals from coming up to have a rootle.

Our personal effects were placed around, and the new bookshelf, running the full width across the back of the van above the bunk bed, was soon filled with our books. The entire length of the hanging cupboard was in danger of being overcrowded by the many garments we jointly owned; and yet it amazed us just how much we did manage to stow away in the caravan's compact space. Each item had to have a specific place for travelling, as in the cabin of a ship. But when we were parked, we could enjoy the lamp on the table and a bunch of fresh wildflowers at the window.

When Dudley placed the Aladdin's lamp, with its smart parchment shade, on the table, covered with its new cloth, the caravan really became home for us. We felt we were ready to start our own nomadic life. The preparations had taken many weeks of thought, hard work and organisation, but the results filled us with such pride and happiness. As we towed the now brilliantly-painted and newly furnished caravan out of the wheelwright's yard, all of our friends there gathered round and gave us a heartening cheer of 'Godspeed and good luck on your travels!'

First Job

Dudley with Benji and Adam

Our first job came to us through the kindness of a friend. A remote dairy farm, belonging to one of the Oxford colleges, needed an odd-job man to help with the milking of a few cows, the feeding of pigs, poultry and calves, and general fieldwork. It sounded just right as a starting point for Dudley, so we gladly accepted the offer. With the caravan all ready to live in, we could start at once.

The farm stood on a high, open ridge of downland, with wide views of Hampshire on one side and Surrey on the other. A long, winding track left the main road at the turnpike and meandered for about a mile through fields and woodland, ending up in the yard outside the farmhouse, where its final tributaries disappeared round the many large and small outbuildings which clustered around the farmhouse like chicks about a mother hen. The whole area was surrounded by large elm trees. They stood like protective presences and gave the feeling of security and goodwill on this high, windy ridge.

Our arrival in the caravan, drawn by the now inevitable noisy tractor, made a tremendous clatter in the otherwise silent atmosphere and caused all the hens scratching in the yard around the big barn to rise up in a cloud of dust, with loud squawks and flying feathers. The bailiff's dogs set up a fierce barking, and a dozen small piglets darted round the barn to peer quickly and then rushed off again, squealing with shrill excitement. Two horses grazing in a meadow came up to the hedge, curious to see the strange cavalcade.

Only the cows in their byre remained quietly chewing their cud, and gently rattling their chains.

The bailiff, alerted by all this commotion, emerged from the barn and eyed the colourful caravan with obvious interest and surprise. Above the din of the tractor, all we could do was to smile in greeting and wave our hands. He came closer and shouted, 'Hello!' We waved again, and he suddenly realized that this was the new odd-job man and his wife, come to work on the farm. The bailiff approached the tractor and shouted the suggestion that the small meadow close to the farmhouse would be a suitable parking place. He then guided us through the gate and Dudley steered the tractor and caravan into position with the caravan's front door facing northeast (from past experience, I had found that this was the best direction for sheltering the entrance from driving rain).

When the tractor's engine was finally switched off, the peace and quiet of the place was intense. The air was still, and we could hear all the small and distant sounds of the far countryside around and below us. It was a blessed quiet, after our noisy journey.

We descended from the tractor and caravan, and stood around stretching ourselves, getting the stiffness out of our limbs and taking in deep breaths of fresh, clean air. The bailiff laughed at our antics.

'Come on in and have some tea,' he said. 'Plenty of time to unpack the caravan afterwards.' Thankfully, I perceived that life up here was taken at a leisurely pace, in keeping with the dignity of the dreaming spires of Oxford!

The old farmhouse was cool and welcoming, with low ceilings, small windows, and many large, dark, exposed beams. A faint, musty smell of plaster, aged woodwork, apples, paraffin, cheese, and tobacco smoke created the atmosphere of a centuries-old farmhouse, which is almost impossible to describe in words. The whole fabric of the building was permeated with generations of human thoughts, emotions and experiences. Time seemed to echo endlessly through its wide passages and largish rooms. There was stillness here and bustle there. But most of all, there was a quiet acceptance of life, which gave it a venerable tranquillity and peace. The very rafters seemed to be whispering, 'All the time in the world. Rest and *be* still.'

During tea, the bailiff talked about some of the previous owners of this old farm. One had a wife who was an expert butter-maker and thought nothing of driving her pony trap each week to the market, over twelve miles away, to sell her precious produce carefully laid out on the cool stone slabs of the Butter Cross. I pictured her travelling the same road as we had come, but under very different conditions: no tarmac road or street lights to help her along; just a muddy and rough track, and then the hard, stone road for ten miles or more, with only her pony for company against all weathers.

After the meal, the bailiff showed us over the place and its buildings, explaining that this was an outlying farm that the college used as a sort of dumping ground for the odd animals that did not fit in their more intensive units. Most of the land was arable, growing corn and root crops to feed the animals on their other stock farms. At the busy harvest and cultivating times, outside labour was brought over from nearby farms to cope with it. But most of the time, it was just a matter of looking after the small number of animals and general maintenance.

The bailiff was also responsible for the other college farms in the area. Consequently, even though he lived in the farmhouse, he was away a great deal, organising and supervising the work of the various units. His great pride was the big pedigree Ayrshire herd on one of these farms. He would dash off early in the morning, often not returning until after dark. As a result, Dudley and I were left very much to our own devices—rather too much, for my liking. The responsibility fell to me to teach Dudley how to milk by hand the four large Ayrshire cows in residence at that time. I think he found their large sweeping horns, shaped like Apollo's lyre, more daunting than their powerful hind legs and swishing tails.

To my delight, the much-prized Ayrshire herd, from which they came, had not been dehorned. This pleased me because the full beauty and dignity of these beasts could be seen and appreciated. The Ayrshires have a particularly pleasing appearance, almost staglike, and they carry their wide horns with real splendour. But, oh, how they could catch one in the ribs. When haltering them in the stalls, they would suddenly toss their heads after taking a quick mouthful from the manger, and land a sharp poke in our ribs (or any other part of our anatomy which was nearest). I suppose this was the price we had to pay for splendour.

Dudley proved an apt pupil, and soon became very proficient with bucket and stool. The milk from the cows was used to feed various weakly calves, who were in need of our special attention, and the remainder went into the mash for the chickens and pigs. We, of course, received our honorary daily pint, as was customary on all dairy farms.

Our life soon followed a familiar pattern of working, eating, and sleeping. My daily 'house chores' in and around the caravan were easy and satisfying to perform. We bought a small oil stove to stand on top of the range, as we found a coal fire too hot in warmer weather. With both of us working outside, the oil stove was quicker for making a hasty midday meal. We also purchased a Cubex oven to fit on top of the oil stove. With this large, biscuit-tin-like device (which proved most useful), we baked excellent cakes, whilst both of us were busy attending to the stock.

For recreation, we frequented a nearby inn. These evening jaunts were both romantic and memorable adventures. Having equipped ourselves with coats and Wellingtons—and a large hurricane lamp—we walked across the meadow to the ridge, along which ran a wide, grassy track. On one side of this track, the land fell sharply away, down into the valley. The slope was heavily wooded in oak, beech, ash, and sycamore. Between the trees, far down below, we could see the high chimneys of the hamlet's cottages. We would then amble along the ridge track for about a mile, where another track veered down steeply through the woodland, coming out into a clearing just above the public house.

The entire hamlet seemed to cling onto the side of the ridge, like a colony of sand martins in a quarry. An ancient Roman road ran up and down the full length of the hamlet. So steep was it, that cars found it almost impossible to negotiate and, therefore, they used only the lower portion. The grey cottages were old and squat, the better to embrace the precipitous slope. The gardens were terraced in careful layers—also to maintain a fierce foothold—and nearly every one of them had a flint retaining wall running round it. In this manner, productive gardens of soft fruits, vegetables, and flowers had been built up by successive generations. Not an inch of precious space was wasted.

Entering the public house was like stepping back into a bygone age. From the ceiling hung oil lamps (the only illumination). The large inglenook fire seemed to burn the year round. The well-worn brick floor of the taproom, as in days of old, was scattered with sawdust to catch drips and spills. In these simple surroundings, we enjoyed many an evening of rollicking songs and such games as darts, skittles, and shove ha'penny.

The company were all locals who worked on neighbouring farms and big estates. Their humour was rich and earthy, like their ready laughter and wit. Their language was Chaucerian by instinct, and full of subtlety. At closing time, after many shouted *good night*'s, followed by various kindly, but ribald, remarks, we would light our hurricane lamp and walk the mile or so, back up through the wood and along the ridge, to the caravan. Sometimes, the stars sparkled more brilliantly than any diamonds, and the moon rode in her high estate, filling the earth with mystery and making us, more than ever, aware of the night sounds all around us—the shrill call of the owls, the sudden and startling flutter of a late-roosting bird, and, occasionally, the sharp, spine-chilling bark of a vixen.

Life on the hill farm was simple and peaceful. We absorbed all of the new sights and sounds, found our way about buildings and fields, and became familiar with the ever-changing collection of animals needing our attention. But, alas, Dudley was not learning any more than I could teach him, and this was only but a small segment of the full range of skills needed to run a farm successfully. He needed more practical experience with operating tractors, learning to plough and cultivate, and, most especially, he needed to join in with the active running of a farm—making decisions, ordering materials, buying and selling stock, and visiting markets. We thought about it and discussed it constantly. This first job had been just right for us, a start to gain confidence and to be sure of the way of life we had chosen. Now that we were sure of our choice, Dudley needed wider horizons in which to hone his skills. And so, we began looking around for a farm offering greater opportunities.

Sadly, we said goodbye to the bailiff, our good friends at the nearby inn, and all of the cows, calves, pigs, hens, and wildlife on this remote hill farm. We packed up the caravan to move along to our next job, which had already been secured by an interview with the owner-farmer who needed a working manager to help generally, as he himself was often away from the farm and required a responsible person in charge. From now on, our farm life was real and in earnest. Dudley got plenty of practice, and soon learned the various fieldwork techniques and the routine with the milking machine. It was a very different life from the serene hill farm and its carefree ways. On this farm, all was business. There were sixty milking cows and their followers, two hundred and fifty acres, six breeding sows and their progeny, *plus* about two hundred laying hens—all to be attended to by the farmer, a full-time general worker, and Dudley. Each time the general worker had his regular half-day off, I helped with the chores.

Granted, we did learn a lot, but we were *not* very happy. The general worker somehow got the idea fixed into his head that we were trying to do him out of a job. Whenever possible, he relayed extravagant and untrue tales about us to the farmer, who, being only human, half-believed them and was, therefore, in a continual state of uncertainty. It made an awkward situation for us all. We tried hard to win the general worker's confidence—some days were happy and the work went easily—but, as the months passed, the good days became few and far between. Endless petty jealousies crept in. Dudley's visits to the market with the farmer were resented and criticised. Even our caravan was suspect. We were foreigners in the camp—seen as the enemy.

In the midst of all this nastiness, we had a lovely surprise: a visit by a friend who was very interested to see the authentic gypsy caravan we lived in. As she was looking it over, she asked, 'Don't you have any lamps for it?' indicating the empty holders on either side of its entrance.

'No, it didn't come with any.'

'Well, I happen to have a pair, which I never use now. You're very welcome to have them.'

Dudley and I agreed that it was a very kind thought, but we never expected to actually receive them. To our great surprise, she returned two days later, proudly bearing two large brass carriage lamps, which fitted perfectly into the brackets, as if they'd been made expressly for them. The lamps did yeoman's service for many years and gave us great pleasure, as such finishing touches often do. Their soft illumination lighted our way, helping to lift our spirits through this dark period.

Finally, the situation became intolerable. It sapped our energy and kept us continually uncertain. All the potential joy and satisfaction in work well done was lost in anxiety. We were hopelessly caught in a black web of envy and mistrust. It nullified every gesture and act of goodwill on our part. So we gave our notice.

Immediately, the atmosphere changed and lightened. The general worker felt victorious and self-justified. The farmer was relieved to see an end to all of the nagging doubts and bad feelings. And, as for us, we were just grateful to be getting away from so much ill will. Commercial farming seemed to be just as bad as big business. We wanted none of it, if it involved this way of living.

During all of this distress, our blessed caravan was a haven of peace and quiet strength. And because its mobility made us independent, we were free to move along just as soon as our week's notice was up. Quietly and quickly, like the Gypsies, we moved away from that unhappy scene, onto the open road, using a hired tractor. By then, it was springtime, and the countryside was brilliantly green. We were so happy to be free from all the disharmony and strife, that we just wandered along for several days, resting our frayed nerves, simply luxuriating in being alive.

It was during this interlude that we happened to meet Alf. He was a tall, wiry, suntanned man who had farmed for many years in the Australian bush. Alf wore the typical slouch hat. All the time we knew him, I hardly ever remember him taking it off. If something bothered or interested him, the hat would be tipped back a few degrees to allow a long, probing forefinger to scratch the crown of his head. Then, with a flip of the same digit, the hat would be eased back into its original position. In bright sunshine, this ubiquitous hat got pulled a few degrees forward, over the long nose and lantern jaw, to shade those deep-set, kindly but keen blue eyes, which never missed a thing!

We took to him at once, and I believe that our unconventional way of living and the fact that we, too, had travelled the world, attracted us to him. He, in turn, was very taken with the caravan. Its mobility appealed to his roving nature. We told him of our recent experiences and troubles. Immediately, he said, 'Come on over and work on my place, why don't you? I'll see you all right.' And so, we did.

It was a wonderfully generous offer. From the moment we towed the caravan up the winding track to his farm, we felt happily at home next to the pond and ready to help out with any jobs which needed doing. Alf's farm was a typical mixed operation, with a few milking cows and their followers, breeding sows and hens, some good arable land, and a lot of rough pasture.

Until our arrival, he did all of the work himself, with only occasional help at harvest time from a local contractor. Having worked for years in the isolation of the Australian bush, Alf was very self-sufficient. He could turn his hand to almost any job, and did it with amazing skill. His methods were unconventional, yet they always worked—often much better than the more elaborate and costly ones advocated by the purveyors of expensive farm equipment. Alf's methods had about them an impressive simplicity. The quality about him which particularly won our hearts was his respect for and love of animals, especially horses. Years earlier, his father had carried quite a name along the south coast of England as a breeder of first-class blood stock, at a time when good horses really were important for work and transport. Alf and his brothers had worked alongside their father from early childhood, picking up all the secrets and tricks of the trade and, above all, learning the true value of a good horse—understanding its delicate nervous system and realising the wonderful response which came when the animal was lovingly and gently handled. The boys learned patience and self-discipline, and were thereby able to break in and train their father's young colts. This early training, severe as it might have appeared to some, had stood Alf in good stead all his life. It gave him a quiet, purposeful dignity which we found very helpful.

To Alf, a farm without a horse was not a farm. Consequently, he kept a lovely mare, which he used for the light harrowing of the fields after drilling, and also in the high hay rake at haymaking time, as well as for various other light jobs. She was a beautiful, shining chestnut, with large, bright eyes and a very shrill voice. Whenever she spotted Alf walking across the meadow towards her, she would canter over to meet him, emitting loud whinnies of welcome and love. She really did love Alf, and would willingly do any amount of work for him. It was a beautiful relationship, with complete understanding between man and mare.

Although Alf's farm was smallish, and the land not the best, he managed to produce some excellent cereal crops, milk, eggs and pigs. He understood all aspects of practical farming. And to us, he was generous with helpful and useful advice. He took Dudley to markets with him and discussed the points to look for and avoid when buying stock. Together, they went to several farm sales to get ideas about the price of second-hand farm machinery. All of this practical help, given so freely by Alf, was of great value to us, as we were beginning to think seriously about finding a place of our own.

At the end of the harvest season, with Alf's full agreement and blessings, we decided the time had come for us to launch out and try our newly won skills on a small holding of our own. One evening, as we were busy searching through newspapers and magazines for advertisements of suitable, small holdings for sale, Alf came over to visit us. He didn't come inside but stood listening to us read aloud various advertisements from the papers. The caravan door was fully open and, standing with his old slouch hat perched at a rakish angle, he suddenly remarked, 'Don't bother with a farmhouse. Just get some good land with suitable buildings, and go on living in this caravan. You will find that a good way to start.' We agreed, but wondered if it would be possible to find good land without a farm-house.

Finding Our Land

Hope with Adam preparing lunch

Sussex is an ancient county, full of unexpected surprises. It has known and tolerated so many different inhabitants—wise Druids, stoical Saxons, proud Romans, crafty Normans—and yet, in spite of all these intrusions, it still keeps its secrets. The long range of downland, running from Folkestone in the East to Portsmouth in the West, is like a high, white-and-green reef, protecting the land and its inhabitants in the deep woodlands and soft valleys that lie behind and beneath. Old pathways, deep tracks, open common land, and vast forests conspire to hold their spells: the simple and magnificent stillness. The ancient magic of Arcadia lingers over the land. Enfolded in this stillness, and close to the Downs, we found our farm, exactly as Alf had prophesied that summer evening by the caravan steps.

In a local paper, the advertisement read:

> *Approx 25 acres of good, light loam, arable and pasture. Excellent buildings. No farmhouse. Land once part of a large estate. Close to downland village.*

We studied it for a long while, wondering, visualising, our imaginations running riot. Could *this* be it? Somehow, it all seemed too easy. 'Let's ask Alf to come and look it over with us,' we both said almost together.

I ran over to his house and showed it to him. He read it slowly and carefully, the long, probing forefinger giving his head an extra scratch, parting the thick-growing hair with an audible swish. 'Yeah, could be the right place,' he said. 'Why don't you two go and have a look at it first, on your own. Then come down and tell me your reactions. If they are good, maybe we will go together and dig deeper. How's that, eh?'

Dudley and I promptly set off for the village post office to telephone and make an appointment to view the property as soon as possible. That evening in the caravan, we got out paper and pencils, sat at the table, and started making plans. With no farmhouse, the land and buildings should not be so expensive. That would leave us more money to spend on stock and implements. We would start with a little dairy herd of pedigree Jersey cows. Their small size would make them easy to handle, with less bulky food in the way of grass and hay required. Although their yield of milk wasn't nearly as great as the Friesian or Ayrshire cow, the extra money received from their high butterfat would help. We might also be tempted to produce cream and butter, as well as milk, for sale.

Jerseys are very much the smallest breed of cow. On their native island home, they are kept almost like a herd of goats, tethered to long chains on ring bolts driven into the ground and moved every so often to new grazing areas. This method takes advantage of every tiny and odd corner of herbage. The animals are closely watched and waited upon by their owners, and become quite tame. I had worked with two Jersey herds during my Relief Milking days, and had found them wonderfully intelligent and friendly. Their long and close contact with man seems to have given them this extra under-standing. Their delicate bone structure, elegant walk, and wonderful liquid-brown eyes, fringed with long, curling black lashes, have given them the title of 'Glamour Girls of the Bovine World.'

We planned to grow fodder crops of sugar beet, cabbage, kale, oats and barley—and to buy the cattle cake necessary for winter feeding. A flock of hens would supply useful cash sales (as well as providing good protein in our own diet).

As our plans evolved, Dudley, with his Economics degree from Cambridge, became absorbed with the financial challenges, while I started weaving mind pictures of beautiful little Jersey cows, contentedly grazing in lush, sunlit pastures, with blue skies above, and a flock of homey hens scratching a cheerful living in the open field, close to their warm and fox-proof houses. The caravan, like the proverbial Good Fairy, sat gracefully at the centre of a secluded, leafy hollow, shedding its beneficent aura of protection all around. The light was golden, the birds sang, the musical plashing of a little stream murmured softly in the background. The air was sweetly scented by the fragrance of wildflowers. So lost was I in this vivid daydream, that when I opened my eyes and glanced out the tiny window, I was quite surprised not to see those Jersey cows, that sparkling sunshine, the babbling brook and the busy brown hens. Dudley—ever the patient, efficient and practical partner—was still engrossed with facts and figures. I felt almost ashamed of my dreamy self. I, too, must try to be practical and realistic.

'How about some supper?' I asked.

'Lovely! I feel like a good fry up.'

As I busied myself preparing a mammoth fry up, he went over his papers and their endless rows of figures just once more, to see how our little nest egg of money could best be put to use.

After dinner and a leisurely stroll in the evening air, we lay in our bunk still discussing our various plans and feeling that, at last, something was going to happen—something important for us. The caravan rocked gently in the breeze. I looked around at its familiar shapes and listened intently to the soft creaking, inside and out. A late-homing blackbird called, an owl hooted in the distance. I was lulled to sleep as the caravan gently swayed.

We were awakened early the next morning by the insistent dawn chorus of birds and the bright shafts of sunlight streaming into the caravan through its tiny windows. We felt oddly different, as if we had moved into another dimension. All of the excitement of the previous evening still lingered with us, and was ever-accelerating now. We looked upon one another with fresh eyes. What a wonderful feeling this anticipation was!

As the kettle slowly came to a boil on the paraffin stove, I placed cups, milk and sugar, bread and butter, and fruit out on the table. 'Let's get on the road well before any other viewers get a chance to put down in an offer ahead of us,' I suggested, a trifle anxious. In my mind's eye, I saw dozens of cars, full of eager purchasers, queued up in front of us. As we ate our breakfast, sunshine filled the caravan, like a good omen. I knew it was going to be another golden day, just like the one when I had found the caravan. I could feel it.

Our drive along the winding Sussex lanes took us through countryside so breathtakingly beautiful that we rode in silence. No words were necessary. This was all part of the magic, the start of our new life. Following the line of the Downs, we drove for several more miles until Dudley pulled the car over into a small lane facing the downland.

'There's the agent's board advertising the property,' he said.

The farmyard to our right was surrounded by a copse of large trees with an undergrowth of hazel and ash. The main buildings were on one side of the yard, facing south. They looked large and strong, but could hardly be called picturesque. Built of wood, they were clad in sheets of thick, corrugated iron. The big yard was large and clean, and the remains of a hayrick stood in one corner.

From one of the buildings came the soft, contented sounds of calves just fed. A man and a woman stood in the yard smiling at us. Getting out of the car, we went over to meet them. They were Noel and Joan Maskelyne, owners of the property, ready to show prospective buyers round the place.

'Mr and Mrs Tod?' the man enquired, holding out his welcoming hand. 'Congratulations! You two are our first viewers of the day.'

We started with the buildings.

'They appear to be strong, but not all that attractive to look at,' Dudley said.

'Their looks belie them,' the owner replied. 'They are beautifully built. Each one is lined throughout with timber, making it warm and draught-proof. Come and have a look.'

The line of buildings started with four large, open-fronted cart sheds. Then came the stables, with standings for three horses. The stalls in the stables had been turned into airy and bright calf pens. Hayracks and bucket stands had been installed in front of each pen. The calves looked healthy and comfortable in their deep beds of straw. As we looked around, they sprawled with stomachs full, looking every bit like an indolent posse of sleek, young pashas awaiting the day's pleasures. Next, there were two large, loose boxes with stable-type doors. They had large windows and good floors, and would make excellent calving pens.

Finally, there was an open-fronted barn for storing hay and straw. It had a foot-high fence at the end, and a gate in front to keep any passing stock in the yard from wandering in and helping themselves to a browse of hay. The Maskelynes were using it as a makeshift milking shed in which to milk their three cows, there being no cowshed or dairy on the premises.

Opposite the stable, on the other side of the yard, was a large pigpen with three separate sties. A cleaning-out passage ran the whole length at the back of the building. In the front, each sty had an external trough and water bowl, so that feeding could be done without entering. There were also metal gates into each sty, giving ready access to the front and rear of the pen. In fine weather, the sow and her litter could lie out in the sty's little yard and enjoy the sunshine and a good feed from the trough, without interference from their neighbours, who could be very aggressive.

As we looked round the yard, we noticed how completely it was surrounded by large elms and oaks, with an undergrowth of hazel and ash, and the single, majestic Scots pine we had seen upon our arrival. Together, they gave the yard a decidedly sheltered and protected feeling, which helped mellow the harshness of the corrugated iron on the buildings.

From the yard, a wide, steep track cut through the copse, leading down to a small meadow surrounded by trees, with a fast-flowing stream chattering through its full length. As we descended into the meadow, my heart began to beat faster. The similarity to the meadow and stream of my mind-picture of the day before was overwhelming: the bright sunlight, the flowing stream, even the sweet-scented wildflowers—everything was there!

It was a rare and exciting recognition. A wide, flat bridge, made out of old railway sleepers, crossed the stream. And the track continued, leading up a slope to a derelict building. Noel informed us that this had once been a mink house, put up by a previous owner who had hoped to make his fortune from selling the pelts of these ferocious little beasts. The entire building had long since collapsed onto its nine-inch-thick concrete slab (a necessary precaution to prevent the imprisoned mink from burrowing to freedom). The slab was surrounded by the largest and darkest green tangle of brambles I had ever seen, caused by the ample amount of mink droppings, no doubt, and their rich, fishy diet, fed in large quantities, to give them glossy coats. Now, all promise of a fortune lay in ruins, with the wild brambles reaping the benefit of the rich manure harvest. Mentally, I envisioned row upon row of pots of dark, red bramble jelly sitting on my storage shelves—quite a different harvest to that envisioned by the previous hopeful owner, but of much greater value to us.

Beyond the 'mink field' (as this area was called) were two more meadows on lower ground. Each led into the other, and both were flanked on one side by a large wood belonging to the neighbouring estate, and by the continuation of the stream on the other.

At one point, beneath a steep bank, the stream became a pond. The Maskelynes told us that, in olden days, bricks had been made in the field next to it, which became known thereafter as Brickfield. On this steep, sandy bank close to the pond were a number of badger setts, obviously in active use because we observed freshly-dug sand scattered near the deep entrances and a large number of footprints on the bank leading down to the water. I was pleased to see that this was a well used area, and I hoped it sheltered several families. I believe badgers are good friends to the farmer. They keep rabbits in check. And if allowed a free run, they will remain in one place for years, giving good service in return for their freedom.

As we continued our walk around the property, we became more and more certain that it was the right place for us. The wildlife would be free to go about its business, and we would try to blend the wild and the cultivated, keeping the natural harmony.

The magical, little meadow next to the pond would be an ideal place for the caravan—close to the buildings, yet masked from the lane by the steep drop in the contour of the land. We would have to build a completely new cowshed and dairy, but this was not a bad thing. It would improve the appearance of the yard to have another building linked with the existing range, and also make attending to the various animals simpler and quicker.

By the time we arrived back in the yard, we had made up our minds. It was definitely the right place for us. Dudley and Noel discussed the terms, and we agreed to make a firm offer and put down a deposit, subject to survey. We realised that a great deal of hard work still had to be done before we could create a small farm out of the present, bare-bones layout. But they were good, strong bones, and we would be able to reconstruct them and fashion new ones, according to our own standards and means, embellishing them as we went along. I thought that a good coat of cream paint on the front, plus bitumen on the roofs, and maybe red paint on the doors would improve their appearance.

During the drive back to Alf's farm, we talked endlessly, planning and rearranging the buildings to include the new cow house and dairy. The vision of the little meadow shone in my memory. It had been such a wonderful confirmation. We were certain that Alf would endorse our decision. The place already had all the essential requirements, including electric lights in the buildings and tap water in the yard. The surroundings were beautiful, and the pastures, which were mostly open, looked to be in reasonable heart. All in all, we felt that we had found solid foundations upon which to build.

Alf's visit the following weekend was a success. He agreed with us and also pointed out that the land, being light loam, would be easy to work, though it would definitely need plenty of farmyard manure and compost to keep it in full production. Alf approved of the buildings, too, and liked the large yard close to the lane, commenting that even in bad winter weather, the milk lorry would be able to call, and we would have no distance to cart the churns. He suggested that a suitable stand could be put up under the large oak tree at the entrance—giving shade to the churns in summer and protection in winter.

Having found our farm, we now bent all our energies and thoughts towards moving in and getting started. Dudley and his solicitor worked hard with pen and paper, drawing up all the necessary contracts and generally tying up all the legal red tape. A satisfactory survey was undertaken, with standing crops included. Since no implements were offered with the sale of the farm, we were free to purchase our own, according to our needs.

True to his word, Alf gave us answers to all the questions we suddenly found filling our minds. He gently cautioned us against over-stocking with mediocre animals in the hope of a quick return, and buying too much equipment.

'Travel light to begin with,' he said. 'Add as you grow, make one implement work where others recommend two. Simplify all the time. In this way, you will gradually accumulate a little extra cash, and will be in a position to buy only quality stock. Good stock is the backbone of a farm, after all. Keep it good and strong, and you will prosper.'

He told us to use as much home-grown fodder as possible and, above all, to keep the land in good heart with organic manure.

'Don't waste your money on artificials and chemicals,' he advised. 'They ruin the soil. Feed yourselves with your own produce. It's the cheapest way to live, and the best.'

I was very mindful of these words later, when we grew fodder beet for the cows and I used the root in salads—finely sliced and dressed with salt, oil, vinegar, and herbs—making a delicious, crisp treat which went well with cold chicken, followed by a thick slice of blackberry-and-apple tart with cream, all from the farm!

The Move

Unidentified caravan admirers pose on the tractor

Our move to the farm took place on a clear and fine September day. We started out very early in the morning, given the thirty-five miles we had to cover, allowing for several rest stops. At our maximum speed (being no greater than five miles an hour), it would take us almost the entire day. After all of our goods were carefully packed away in the caravan, and we'd cleaned up the site where we had so happily rested during our stay on Alf's farm, I went down to the buildings to say goodbye to the cows I had so often milked.

As I entered the cowshed, large, understanding eyes followed me silently as I moved about. I talked to each animal in turn, caressing their coats and saying my farewells. The old herd leader, Flossie, a gentle shorthorn of advanced years, licked my hand with her raspy tongue, and then gently nudged me with her head. She had often helped me by leading the herd directly up to the gate nearest the cowshed and, as I opened it, marching them through with a loud bellow, as if to say, 'Follow on behind me now, and get into your shed without dawdling.' How meekly they all obeyed this wise, old matriarch, each one seeming to know by instinct her place in the herd. But woe betide any young greenhorn who dared to jump the queue! In an instant, Flossie's gentle, easygoing nature changed, and the foolish upstart was sharply butted back to her place in line. Flossie was the boss.

After the cows, I visited the little calves. They rushed up to me, thinking perhaps I had brought them an extra feed. They licked at my fingers hopefully, tugging to try and draw milk from these teat-like objects, their tails thrumming rhythmically against their tiny flanks, as they tussled and sucked. I bent down and kissed their soft, little heads, and then withdrew my fingers from their eager, trusting mouths. Disappointed, they skipped away, to play with each other, chasing the patches of sunlight.

Finally, I went over to the pigpens to give the sows a farewell scratch behind their ears. They grunted their goodbyes and looked straight into my eyes (as pigs will do) with their clear, knowing gazes. For an instant, my mind flashed back to the earliest days of man's association with swine. Together, they had roamed the forests seeking food and shelter, each one contributing to the others' well being. The sight of Alf's contented creatures confirmed the continuing progress that had been made over the centuries in their relationships. It was a good feeling to experience. All of the beasts to whom I had just bid farewell were, I knew, safe in Alf's kind and capable care, so I left them without too much sorrow.

Hurrying back to the caravan, I found Dudley busy coupling it to the tractor. I mounted the step via the coupling hook, and took up my position at the open door. Alf piloted us down his long track and stood, slouch hat well forward, to watch us pull out into the road. This manoeuvre safely accomplished, he gave us a final wave of his hand and then turned. The parting had been made easier by his promise to come over and visit us, as soon as we had settled.

Travelling at five miles an hour in a high vehicle, such as our gypsy caravan, is a wonderful opportunity for surveying the passing landscape. As we progressed on our slow journey, I found myself able to look over the tall hedges into otherwise secret gardens, known only to their owners, who lived private lives outdoors. And, as we passed by, I could look through the upstairs windows whose curtains were drawn, revealing interiors scattered with personal possessions, unmade beds, discarded clothing, boxes, chamber pots, and, in one room, a couple lying naked on a large bed, quite lost to the goings-on in the outside world.

In roadside farms, I saw stock resting comfortably in covered yards; backdoor steps behind high, brick walls, where small children were safely at play with their toys; cats basking in the early autumn sunshine, like small tigers in a tropical setting, all the colours flashing and sparkling in the morning light; gardens full of flowers, vegetables, and fruit trees spilling their bounty all around them. Trees, meadows, and recently ploughed fields made a beautiful patchwork pattern. The bright sky was reflected in large, clear ponds, and the rivers we passed flowed in sinuous curves, reminiscent of silver snakes crawling across the green landscape.

Our passage through towns caused quite a stir, and Dudley had to keep a sharp lookout for sudden turns, one-way streets, blind alleys, shop and inn signs hanging out over the roadway, and small children darting off the pavements to have just one more look at the gypsy caravan.

We halted several times, drawing onto the side of the road or a lay-by to have a stretch and chat, check the wheels for overheating, and to shut off the infernal noise of the tractor. Our longest stop was for the midday meal, which we planned to eat inside the caravan, so that Dudley could rest his long legs on the sofa. We happened to choose as our stopping place one of several lodged entrances to a large estate, since the space was wide and conveniently just off the main road. Just as we started to enjoy our meal, an anxious little man wearing bedroom slippers, dark trousers, a white shirt and plum coloured waistcoat with shining brass buttons all down the front, popped suddenly out of the lodge to demand haughtily and loudly whether we were stopping for long. Dudley rose from his comfortable position on the sofa and descended from the caravan. His size, polite voice and upright bearing completely bewildered the huffy little man, who—after several startled 'Oh, I see, sir,' 'That's quite alright, sir'—popped back into his lodge like Alice's rabbit in Wonderland. I suppose he feared we were real Gypsies, and that his lordly master would not care to see such vagrants drawn up outside one of the approaches to his grand park.

Accordingly, we were very careful to leave no rubbish behind us—not even the smallest pool of tractor oil to soil our temporary resting place. We left it as spotlessly clean as it had been on our arrival. And as Dudley pulled out onto the road again, I looked back through one of the caravan's windows and saw the lodge window curtain twitch slightly, and then fall back into place. Obviously, our departure had been observed and noted with relief!

As we approached our newfound farm, I began to look more closely around me. We had passed through the lower part of the downland village and out onto a narrow, winding lane. The farm would be about one and a half miles beyond the village. This pleased me—to know that we were not right inside it, but slightly removed. As we wound our way along the lane, I noticed how the landscape undulated quite steeply, yet the clear line of the Downs could always be discerned as a beautiful backdrop to the daily life of the forests, meadows, and fields. This lane leading to our farm was, indeed, like 'the rolling English road' in G. K. Chesterton's poem. Its delicate curves were as satisfying to the mind as they were to the eye.

Over a small hill, there was the farm on our left-hand side. Slowly, we entered the large yard between the big oak on our left and the Jacobean Scots pine on our right. With great care, Dudley drove across the yard and down the copse cutting into the magical little meadow with the stream. We found a level piece of ground and angled the caravan so that the door was facing northeast, uphill towards the yard. We uncoupled the tractor and drove it back up the hill into the yard, placing it in one of the open cart sheds. As we were walking back down the copse cutting, we looked into the meadow. The caravan sat there contentedly, basking in the rays of the setting sun, its beautiful shape and gay colours blending into the surroundings so perfectly that it was a joy to behold. We looked up into the surrounding trees and the sky beyond, and felt quite overcome at being the owners of so much natural beauty. With infinite pleasure and satisfaction, we mounted the steps and entered our home to brew ourselves a welcome cup of tea.

The evening sunlight, slanting in through the windows, was mellow and welcoming. At length, we stirred ourselves and began to unpack and prepare for the night. Whilst we were busy at our allotted tasks, we heard a knock on the side of the caravan. I saw the Maskelynes (who lived in a cottage up the lane) standing by the steps looking up at us, holding in their hands a jug of milk and a bowl of eggs. 'We thought you might find these useful,' he said. 'Please let us provide you with milk and eggs until you get going.'

Their simple act of thoughtful kindness was such a benediction.

'We won't stay,' he added. 'You must both be very tired after that long journey. Good night, and may you sleep well.' With these words, they turned and hurried back up the copse cutting, through the yard, and into the lane.

'What a lovely beginning to our life here,' I said to Dudley. And as he smiled, the clear notes of a robin sounded in the copse—Nature's symbolic welcome!

As the light slowly faded, we completed our final tasks. Holding a nightcap of cocoa in our hands, we sat on the step board and listened to all the new sounds around us. One of the loveliest was the little stream chattering its way down from the hills.

Adam's Farm

Open-front sheds (top) and Green Horn's garage

The early morning light awoke us. We were soon up and moving around, lighting the stove, preparing breakfast and making coffee. It was a beautiful day, with warm sunshine and a clear blue sky. I heard the cooing of wood pigeons, looked at Dudley, and said with a big smile, 'You were right, darling. This all seems so perfect to me.'

As we were tidying up, I heard the Maskelynes arriving with fresh eggs and milk for us, as promised. How thoughtful they were! I came down the steps to welcome them. 'Noel has something to show you,' Joan said. 'If you are ready, we could show you now.'

So off we went to the far end of the meadow, where a small plank bridge across the stream led into the copse with two ponds, and then to a larger pond. High banks on our right led up into the top field. There was a path next to the ponds and much reed grass, all surrounded by overhanging trees.

'What a beautiful spot,' I said.

Then Noel stood still and studied the water in one of the small ponds. 'Look! Do you see him?'

I looked and saw a huge, gold fish swimming slowly around in lazy circles. 'It's a real fish,' I whispered. 'Goodness! How did *he* ever get there?'

'I put him there, years ago,' Noel explained.

'Does it have a meaning?'

'I belong to the Magic Maskelyne Devant[*] family,' he continued. 'I enjoyed doing things like this in the old Egyptian Hall in
London.'

If this was supposed to be his explanation, neither Dudley nor I
understood it. 'How wonderful,' I exclaimed, at a loss for words.
'We will take good care of him, I promise.'

'Thank you for introducing him to us,' Dudley said. 'He really
is quite a beautiful golden fish.'

Pleased on hearing this, Noel smiled and said, 'I'm glad you
like him, too, and that you understand why I placed him here. But
now, I suspect that you both are eager to start on your journey of
discovery around the farm?'

We agreed, so they retraced their steps back up into the farmyard. We watched them until they disappeared through the trees.
'How amazing,' Dudley said, 'to think that we've bought the farm
that used to belong to the Magic Man himself. It really is right.
What a fine start to our day of discovery here.'

We passed by the big pond and came out into the lower field.
The grass there was green and even, and since the field was long
and narrow, with the surrounding trees, it looked to me very much
like a polo field. I asked Dudley, 'Shall we call it the "polo field"?'

'Why, yes, that's a fitting name for it.'

All along our bounty line was an arboretum known as Topley
Ridge, which rose up and up, with multicoloured foliage. It was
spectacular. We reached the far end of the polo field, turned to the
right, and opened a gate which led up into the top fields. The hedge-

---

[*] John Nevil Maskelyne (1839-1917) was one of the greatest British magicians. He ran the Egyptian
Hall in Piccadilly with his son, Nevil Maskelyne. David Devant (1868-1941), born David Wighton,
joined the Hall's illusionist show in 1893, and later became part of the very successful Maskelyne-
Devant team.

rows along the lane were thick, high, and filled with wildflowers and herbs growing in the sun. The branches of the overhanging hedgerow trees provided filtered shade. The combined scent of the various herbs delighted me. 'A wonderful pasture for Jersey cows,' I remarked out loud and then stopped.

Immediately, Dudley was close by me, his eyes shining. 'I would love to have them here, too. They are so small, delicate and friendly.'

We joined hands and slowly roamed the field, exploring the magical hedgerows, envisioning our small herd of Jersey cows grazing contentedly in this very pasture, and producing rich, creamy milk. When we crested the top of the ridge, we stopped yet again to take in the noble sweep of the South Downs spread before us in their splendour and vastness.

'I wonder,' I said, 'if we still retain grazing rights up there on the hills? I know that, in olden days, it was so. But perhaps it is all different now.'

On the crown of the hill was another gate, which opened onto the lane, so we passed through it and wandered down to the farmyard. In their peaceful setting, the buildings looked fine and strong. I now felt much more in tune with them, and their beautiful ring of trees.

'Do you think the Scots Pine has any history connected with the Jacobites?' I said. 'They always planted a Scots Pine tree as a sign.'

'It could be a sign to travellers in the olden days of deep snow,' Dudley said, 'a sign that they could get help here, if they were benighted.'

Dudley was already busy investigating the four big bays on our right as we entered the yard. 'Plenty of space to store hay and straw, as well as various implements,' he said.

Next, we stood in the centre of the yard and looked around carefully. 'The cowshed would be exactly right for the far end of the yard,' he said. 'Plenty of room for the Jerseys to go in and out with ease. They do love to waltz mincingly along, don't they?'

I laughed at this delicious idea of cows waltzing. They do move so beautifully and with such grace. 'We will need to put in a boiler house at the rear so we can have a real bath once a week!'

Our two dogs, which had been following us around the farm, came close to us now and looked up with hungry expressions. 'Guess it must be time for dinner,' I called out loudly, and they leapt up and started running down the track towards the van. We followed them, and I soon had a meal on the table for us, while the dogs enjoyed their dinner under the van, as usual.

At last, silent contentment filled the air. Just the little stream, softly bubbling along on its endless journey, with the hypnotic sound of water moving over stones—the only sound to be heard for quite a while. Then the dogs began stirring, their stomachs full, ready for more adventuring and discovery. Adam, the male, mixed-breed 'Pi' dog we had brought back with us from India, hopped up the steps and gazed at us with his head cocked to one side, as if to say, 'Well, where shall we go next?'

We both looked back at him and smiled. He was such a gentle soul, always ready to join in with whatever we planned to do, or just go off on his own. As I watched his alert, brown eyes, I said, 'We have to give our farm a name, so shall we call it Adam's Farm?'

Dudley, who had been lying back on the bed, sat up, surprised at my sudden outburst. Adam put his two front paws up on the bed and looked at Dudley with great earnestness.

'It's an easy name,' Dudley said. 'Very well. From now on, we will be known as Adam's Farm, Graffham, near Petworth, in the County of West Sussex.'

Benji, our other dog, whom we had inherited from Alf, gave a little bark from under the van. To our ears, it sounded like a small bark of approval. I went down the steps and gave him a hug. It was the generosity of his youthful nature to accept that Adam was the first and most important. Benji was, after all, just a little brother, and contented to be so.

During our earlier walk about the farm, we hadn't fully explored the high ground on the other side of the stream. It was marked as 'Round Wood Copse' on the map, and was a wild part, with much bracken growing along the boundary. We crossed the little stream by the low, wide bridge which neatly spanned it, and moved up into the bracken. In the middle of it, we saw the large slab of concrete we'd seen earlier, quite surrounded by blackberry bushes. How kindly Nature deals with man's eager greed to make a quick buck.

We stood on the slab and looked downward, into the meadow containing our beautifully coloured van. They made a lovely picture in the afternoon sunlight. We continued walking up to the Round Wood Copse and admired the trees which were mostly chestnuts, then with only green leaves fluttering in the breeze. Adjacent to the copse was our bounty with a post-and-rail fence against intruders. As we stood at the top of the Round Wood Copse, we could see the full length of the polo field stretching out before us, with the three ponds on our right and the top fields just above, showing between the hedges. It was a beautifully compact little farm on three levels, with infinite variety in its ups and downs—its ponds and stream and pastures all so well sheltered against the vigorous winds that blew out of the southwest in certain seasons.

We talked about such practicalities as what sort of animals we wanted and which style of farming we wished to follow. But we knew that our first priority was to clean the buildings—the two big, loose boxes, and the barn and stables. None of them had been in active use for some time, since Noel and Joan had done their chicken rearing closer to their cottage, and they had kept just one 'house cow,' who now lived in the little meadow on the other side of the lane.

There had been a few calves in the end stall of the stables that had already been sold. All that remained from these activities were the wooden railings which had kept them safe inside the stable, and three wooden frames to hold their buckets of milk. We decided to fill the four big bays beside the stable with oat straw, when we could find some locally. Dudley wanted to use one of the bays as a space for the car, so essential for travelling to and fro, seeking out and finding livestock, oat straw, and so on. So the first bay beside the stable became 'Green Horn's Garage,' named after our car.

When we opened the first loose box, wondering what we would find, we discovered that it was completely empty, but festooned with the most enormous spider webs I had ever seen, dangling from the rafters high above. They were a striking sight to behold, shimmering beautifully in the sunlight that came streaming in through the window and the half-open stable door. I felt a real sense of regret and loss as I swept them all down with a long-handled broom. So much work had gone into spinning their geometric shapes. They reminded me of those I had seen on one of the farms where I'd worked, literally covering the whole six-acre pasture in the early mornings. Those had been low, just at grass-top level, creating the impression of a billowing veil, or a gossamer net of light, all across the entire expanse of the field. They were so delicate, and yet, so strong, that they could lift off into the air with the slightest breeze and move with amazing speed—a real miracle of Nature.

The spider webs in the loose box, on the other hand, made a large heap on the confined space of the stone floor as I swept them down. And, as soon as they were splashed with water, they quite suddenly disappeared into filmy nothingness.

Our respect for the buildings grew progressively as we worked our way through each of them. They were so well built, constructed as they were from double, heavy-duty, corrugated iron sheeting, completely lined with wood, from top to bottom, plus wooden rafters, doors, and window frames. Underfoot was an even stone floor, comprised of small, square granite blocks, neatly fitted. In fact, Lord Woolavington (the estate owner) had occasionally kept two of his racing mares with their foals in these same boxes. The farmer had been one of his tenants who obliged and, as a result, had the very finest materials to construct his buildings with.

For several days, we swept and washed and scrubbed, gradually getting the whole range of buildings beautifully clean and fresh once more, ready to receive their new occupants.

The centre loose box we decided to turn into a feed storage area and a general farm office, complete with a telephone. We had to have somewhere for reps who came with deliveries, and we wanted to keep the van as our very private home, separate and out of sight from the yard. Having a telephone on the farm was a necessary luxury, as we had none in the caravan, and it proved to be extremely useful in making all sorts of different contacts and ordering various supplies. I did understand its true value, and so did Dudley, who started making phone calls as soon as the instrument was installed, saving us innumerable trips into town. He was particularly eager to procure some good quality oat straw. This he was easily able to accomplish by simply phoning Jesse Hill at a nearby farm, who grew organic straw in the real old-fashioned way: he had one son working with him, and they did everything together in the simplest possible manner. Dudley was so impressed with the quality of their oat straw that he even brought a bale home in the car! I gazed at it with sheer delight. It was, indeed, golden in colour, with firm stems, and the scent from it was truly aromatic. I was certain that the Jersey cows would love it.

Dudley told me all about his visit to Jesse Hill's farm. They had two Jersey house cows they had been milking steadily for two years, without having to put them to the bull. They produced enough for their daily use and for the poultry feed, mixed with their home-grown oats and corn, as well as having some for the pigs they also kept. Theirs was a timeless farm with an easy, gentle rhythm, which kept them working—but not too hard—with plenty of time left to stand and stare and talk about the weather, their crops, and their Jersey cows. Dudley was quite fascinated by what he had seen and heard during his visit, and I, too, very much enjoyed hearing all about it. It seemed that the joy and delight spread itself out, expanding and expanding, to include the whole farm and all its occupants.

Jesse Hill understood the true meaning of farm life: nothing was wasted, nothing was exploited.

To become farmers ourselves, we needed stock purchased not at market, but individually chosen from small herds of pedigree Jerseys. This proved to be much more time-consuming, yet infinitely wiser, for our way of life.

The Cows

Ecclesden Delinquent

The first little cow we found had been given the unfortunate name of Ecclesden Delinquent. She came from a small herd of pedigree Jerseys not far from Petworth. Her owner, a young woman of twenty, was getting married, and wished to sell the animals privately. We drove over to meet her and look at her six pedigree cows. They were a very contented little herd, lovingly cared for. Immediately we saw Ecclesden Delinquent, we knew she was right for us. She had a lovely golden coat and mealy-coloured nose, huge dark eyes with long, long lashes, two tiny horns and the graceful walk of a Hartnell[*] model. She stepped so daintily and carefully with her four black hooves, that I named her My Lady Pussy Foot (which later became simply Pussy). We completed our purchase, took her official pedigree and papers home with us to study at our leisure, and arranged transport to Adam's Farm in a small horse box.

A week later, Pussy was installed in the end bay, where there were three neck chains and a long manger with plenty of straw to lie on. She was extremely comfortable and milked well without any problems. Our small meadow was large enough for her on her own, with our company in the van nearby, though we did have to put a rail fence round the van for safety and convenience, after she came to nudge the van out of curiosity.

Another advertisement sent us seeking a companion for Pussy, Pulborough way. Again, it was a small herd selling privately. The

---

[*] Fashion designer Norman Hartnell (1901-1979).

Jersey was named Stella: a lighter colour than Pussy, but very gentle and friendly, with an excellent, straight back and good carriage. As soon as she arrived, both animals became good friends and companions, sharing the long manger, with Stella happily yoked up beside Pussy for milking. It was so good to finally have two little Jerseys.

And so, very gradually, our little herd grew. Meanwhile, all the plans for the new dairy and cowshed were carefully drawn up by Dudley and an architect friend—and the builders had started their work. The pattern of the masons' brickwork fascinated me. From a single line, they progressed row by row, gradually transforming a pile of bricks, as if by magic, into the ten stalls of our new dairy adjoining the cowshed by a double door. Each cow would have her own individual standing with a comfortable yoke, a drinking bowl, and her own manger (so no stealing of each other's food could go on). A wide passage at the front of the mangers enabled us to easily distribute cake straw and cabbage feed with a wheelbarrow, dishing out food in exact quantities required by each cow. Big windows, on either side of the shed, provided plenty of natural light. A wide dung passage, with a broad walkway running the full length of the building, made the task of cleaning out easy. All was tailor-made for the Jersey cows' comfort.

At the end of the shed was the dairy, fully equipped with two washing troughs, shelving for the buckets, and the cooling plant, where the milk flowed over directly into the churn to chill it to the correct temperature. Everything was well organised and easy to operate. The electric milking clusters also had their appointed places on fixtures mounted to the wall.

When all was complete, it really did look splendid, with the fresh, white walls set off by scarlet doors. As each new cow arrived, I carefully hand-painted a name plate for her in the classic style of lettering, and then affixed it to a metal plate mounted above her head on the top rail that ran the length of the shed. On the back wall, there was a shelf for the Milk Marketing Board's record sheets, for keeping track of each cow's yield. Nothing was overlooked. It was really a pleasure to milk in such a parlour, which was light, airy, and dry, and quite comfortable, even in the worst winter weather.

The dairy and cowshed had separate entrances, with the motors for the boiler and milking machine in a room apart, to reduce the noise as we milked with the Alfa Laval milking units. The boiler supplied hot water for washing up the utensils, etc. Electric power was taken to the cowshed from the main building which already had light and power points. It was wonderful the way in which each section linked up into one whole. The yard really was a yard now, with buildings on each side and at the end. The broad concrete walkway outside the cowshed and dairy kept our feet very clean and comfortable. We were making progress! We decided to purchase our third cow and then move them all into their beautiful, new quarters.

Her name was Lily's Pride 39th, and she came from the largest and most important pedigree herd of Jerseys in the country at that time. The manager said they wanted to sell her because she was too slow and stupid. And as the odd one out, Lily's Pride 39th didn't seem to fit in with the other milkers of that herd. Still, I loved her as soon as I saw her. Her coat was a pale golden colour. She had big, dark eyes with typical, long, thick, lashes; a mealy nose; beautifully shaped little horns that curled inwards; black hooves; and a particularly long tail with a dark tip which, when washed and brushed, swished about in a most aristocratic manner. Like all Jerseys, Pussy and Stella also had long tails, ending with the characteristic wide, dark strands that gave them a dramatic finish as they swayed along into the cowshed. They all put their tails to good use in summer, to repel vicious flies.

Lily's Pride 39th was large for a Jersey—much larger than either Pussy or Stella—but very gentle and almost fearful of the quick movement of the others around her. Although she was slow, and a bit awkward, in my experience, she was not stupid. Dudley and I felt that, in our tiny herd of hand-picked cows, she would fit in better—which she did, as it turned out. And since the records showed that her milk yield was also very high, in both quantity and quality, we decided to purchase her and have her delivered to Adam's Farm as soon as possible.

We chose a quiet autumn day to move them all into their new home. I was nervous, because we planned to use the rubber-lined teat cups of our new Alfa Laval milking unit on them for the first time, and Pussy and Stella had only been hand-milked up until this point. We brought them into the shed slowly, and allowed them a while to eat some food before turning on the milking machine. We talked to them all the time in a quiet voice and then gently slipped the rubber-mounted teat cups onto each teat, one at a time. Stepping back, we held our breaths, waiting to see how they reacted. Pussy looked round and then simply went on eating her nuts. Stella's reaction was similar, except she couldn't even be bothered to look around. Of course, Lily's Pride 39th was already accustomed to machine milking. We were relieved that all went well. We monitored the process carefully, keeping an eye on the milk flow, and then did a final, gentle stripping out of the teats, to make sure all the milk had been gotten out, before switching off the machine and moving on to the next cow.

When we removed the four cups, Pussy and Stella swished their tails and started eating again. I felt like doing a little jig in celebration and shouting 'Hurrah,' but knew that I must keep very quiet and calm, patting their flanks in an admiring way, with lots of caressing words, which Pussy, especially, loved to hear. It had all been so much easier than we had anticipated. That evening in the van, Dudley and I broke out a bottle of wine to celebrate. Now, we were ready to find some more Jerseys.

Our next cow, named Snailwell Royal Empress, belonged to a couple who each had somehow lost the sight in one eye. She had lost her sight in the left eye and her husband in his right. The wife remarked to me, when we went to visit them, 'If we stand together, we have one good pair of eyes between us to examine an animal!' They were such nice people, and so interested in what we were trying to build up: a herd of pedigree Jerseys. They took a great deal of care to ensure that we received all of Snailwell Royal Empress's papers—pedigree, age, number of calves she'd had, and a vet's certificate of her soundness. She soon joined us, and happily settled in with Pussy, Stella, and Lily's Pride 39th.

Our fifth cow, Highland Cute Pet, was another one who came to us from the same, large, pedigree herd where we had found Lily's Pride 39th. Our numbers were steadily increasing. We now needed an official outlet for our Jersey milk, which carried a premium on its butterfat content.

The day before the man from the Milk Marketing Board came to visit us, I bought a small tin of condensed milk for his tea. I could *hardly* give him a cup of tea made with our cows' milk, since we were not yet officially registered as milk producers. However, he was very impressed with our lovely new cowshed and dairy. After examining our five cows, he announced, 'Congratulations, Mr and Mrs Tod. You are now officially registered as milk producers.' He gave us the necessary forms for recording each cow's yield (mornings and evenings) and told us that, once a month, a man called the Milk Recorder would come and check that the milk and the yields recorded on the sheets were correct.

At the entrance to the farm, we constructed a suitable stand (as Alf had suggested) of exactly the right height for the milk churns to rest on until the milk lorry called for them each morning at our appointed pick-up time. Now we *really* had a discipline to follow, like it or not: twice-daily milkings, seven days a week, at 6 A.M. and 6 P.M. We were in business!

Autumn was coming to the South Downs. We already had a good supply of Jesse Hill's excellent oat straw, and a whole rick of fresh meadow hay standing in the top field, which we had purchased from the Maskelynes when we bought the farm. Each month, we purchased dairy nuts from the corn chandler's in Midhurst, building up our supply in the farm office for the coming winter months. Jerseys are particularly fond of cabbage and sugar beet. But since we were too late in the year for these crops, we planned carefully to include them with the following spring's planting. There was plenty of good pasture, which would tide us over the first winter.

Every day, we groomed our cows before each milking (with a long-bristled dandy brush and a steel currycomb) until their coats shone with a glorious glossy glow. It pleased us to no end to see how much they, too, seemed to enjoy this attention. We also liked grooming their mealy-coloured noses. Their enormous, dark eyes would shine with pleasure, thanking us for all our efforts. These were animals who, for many centuries, had been closely handled on their island home, often wearing specially-made jackets to protect their silken coats. They were led about Jersey Island fields with halters on a long rope, often tethered, to conserve the scarce turf they consumed. In contrast, we had plenty of space, so we allowed ours complete freedom of movement; and they, as a result, rewarded us with excellent yields with high butterfat content.

They were so tame, gentle and friendly, we came to love them dearly. Each had her own distinctive ways of expressing her feelings and preferences for particular foods. As we stood at the field gate watching them, morning and evening, they always fascinated us. Looking up from their grazing, they would recognize the call, and then come eagerly towards the gate, swishing their tails, glad of the anticipation of nuts and hay, and to be relieved of their heavy yield. Our journeys to and from the fields were invariably enhanced by some little action of one cow or another—either gently pushing forward, in eagerness to reach the cowshed and fresh food, or on the return journey, hurrying on to a particular part of the meadow to be the first to relish some delectable, newly-discovered herbage, growing in profusion in a certain place. In all seasons, our little herd kept us constantly entertained and amused with their delicious, individual quirks and antics. The reason they responded so well to us, I am quite sure, was because they felt safe and cared for, in ways they understood.

The Hens

Dudley with Benji in front of the fold units

Our next venture was poultry and the production of eggs. But before we could get started on this particular project, we urgently needed a small tractor—to move hay and straw, harrow the meadows, and generally fetch and carry. Dudley found a splendid little Massey-Harris Ferguson tractor in a contractor's yard in Chichester. It was just right for us, and very reasonably priced, so Dudley bought it outright, the contractor kindly offering to transport it to the farm the next day. The tractor fitted neatly into one of the four bays at the entrance to the farm. So now we had two essential machines: a car and a tractor.

We talked long and hard about the best way of keeping hens. We wanted free-range style in the field, so we decided to try innovative fold units which were complete, moveable poultry houses—with nesting boxes, a run, food trough, and a wire cover to protect the birds from predators such as foxes. The units could be easily moved daily onto a fresh patch of pasture. They enabled the hens to live together in harmony, and the pasture to evenly benefit from the birds' droppings. Since our soil was light loam (as Alf had told us), it needed generous enrichment and consolidation. It seemed the perfect solution for so many of our problems.

A farm near Chichester advertised these large, light fold units for sale. We visited the farm to see them in operation and were very impressed. The units incorporated all that we were looking for: lightness and strength, with complete safety for the hens. Two people could move them daily, one at each end holding the wooden handles, moving each unit one full length, thereby slowly progressing across the entire pasture, eliminating cleanout and controlling the use of the pasture at the same time. We ordered two of the units.

When they arrived within the week on a huge, long lorry with a low chassis, we asked for them to be deposited inside the lane gate at the top field. I was amazed at how light they actually were in relation to their size. But once on the ground, they were really firm, due to the attached anchoring stakes which we pushed into the soil. Covered at the rear end of each unit were the nesting boxes and perches, with a drop stick to close the door into the run at night, and keep the hens safe inside.

Now that we had the houses for the poultry, we could go ahead and buy some laying hens. Noel Maskelyne was very interested in our solution for keeping hens 'on the hoof,' as he called it. He examined the units so carefully and so thoroughly, I became anxious, in case there was something missing. He smiled as he looked at them and said, 'I am fascinated by them. They are *so* complete. I wish I'd thought of designing them myself.' This was praise, indeed, coming from a magician. He was so interested in seeing how they worked that we promised to give him a demonstration when the hens arrived. Through his contacts with his day-old chick business, and his quick eye for suitable layers, we felt very sure that all would be well for our little flock. A week later, Dudley went over with the car to a nearby poultry farm to collect our Rhode Island Red, North Holland Blue, and White Wyandotte layers. In the future, we would hatch our own replacements, or buy them from the Magic Man himself.

The Pigs

Wessex Saddleback sows

Our farm was steadily growing around us. All that was missing were the pigs. With pigs in the sties, we would finally have a farm of mixed animals—what I had always dreamt of, and so had Dudley. Being able to work together all day, and then to enjoy the evening in our warm van with the dogs, made life wondrously sweet for both of us.

The arrival of our first pigs was an unexpected surprise. They were two large Wessex Saddleback sows belonging to a couple who had sidetracked into breeding beautiful (but temperamental) Afghan hounds. The dogs were selling extremely well—so much so, that the pigs had to go! Their owners had neither the space nor the time to look after them properly any more, so the pigs came to us, and we were delighted to have them.

The morning they arrived, in a trailer hitched to their owners' car, I noticed that autumn was approaching in earnest. There was crispness in the air. Graffham Down, at whose foot our farm lay, often had a misty haze on the high ground. Colours were beginning to change on the trees. The full autumn glory was slowly coming into its own. The beauty of it all was a continual delight. The beech copse, behind the pigsties and at the end of the cowshed, suddenly turned pale gold in the full sun, and the leaves rustled in the breeze. Soon they would start to fall, and the downland would become visible through thin, naked branches. The great Scots pine remained dark green, as always, all year round. The cows came in eagerly for the evening milking, and grew increasingly reluctant to return to the field. Soon they would be lying in at night, snug in their beautiful new house, and resting comfortably on deep beds of wheat straw litter, safe from wind and weather. The milk stand—which, after all, carried most of our farm's income—was checked regularly, to ensure that it hadn't been knocked cockeyed again by the milk lorry. And the hens were happily settled in, finally rewarding us with their bounty of beautiful big eggs, safe in their units, which we always moved daily, up and down the field, manuring it with just the right quantity.

Autumn & Winter at Adam's Farm

And having laid her eggs she thinks no harm
To sit alone all day and keep them warm.
When men with carts come by, or lurching cows,
Or shrieking children shake the willow-boughs,
Like formless shadows on a lighted blind
Anonymous terror moves across her mind,
And yet, for good or ill,
She's patient even so, and holds her still.

— *From* The Moorhen, *by Gerald Bullett*
Poems in Pencil, 1937

Cosy caravan's first snow at Adam's Farm

As Dudley and I moved around the yard and the fields, we noticed the subtle changes. I began to think of storing dry wood for the daily lighting of the van's coal fire. Each week, I ordered a few extra tins of food to stock up our cupboard for the winter months. We installed a paraffin drum in one of the sheds to refill the bottles for our heater, cooker, and the lamps. I attended to our Elsan lavatory behind the big barn with the mixture we got in from our supplier, making sure that the door fitted well and that plenty of paper was available. Feed corn and dairy nuts were regularly ordered, and the bales of Jesse Hill's beautiful oat and wheat straw were carefully counted and placed neatly in the big open bay.

When our duties were completed each day, we retired to the warm, fire-lit van with a lamp upon the table and a hot meal on the stove. Adam and Benji slept in the office in the yard, on guard against any unwanted late-night travellers. We were all in our appointed places, secure in the knowledge that all was well. As Dudley and I happily folded together in our fairytale farmhouse on wheels, the night owls called as they hunted the voles and the mice, and we listened to their movements in the trees, close by. All the while, the little stream maintained its gentle burbling sound, with the meadow sheltering us all as we slept peacefully in these primordial natural surroundings.

In the middle of October, for the first time, our cows stayed in all night. The day had been miserably wet, and by evening the sodden field was no longer a comfortable place for them. We also knew that the hooves of the little Jerseys would 'poach' the soft turf—which would not be good for man nor beast. With this in mind, we had already made preparations for keeping them in: two bales of wheat straw were at the back of the cowshed, for bedding, and more feed hay was ready in the front passage. As soon as we got them safely into their stalls, we had to groom them thoroughly, carefully wiping their udders with a warm, damp cloth, and gently massaging them to ease the milk flow. Next, continuing with the usual routine, we turned on the machine and started milking. They responded surprisingly well, feeling comfortable and cared for. With the milking behind us—and the engine turned off, the utensils washed clean in cold and then warm water—I stood a moment, observing our now settled and beautifully groomed cows. How lovely they were.

Pussy turned her head and looked at me, rather questioningly. The rain was pounding on the roof and the wind was streaking through the half-open door. Taking this all in, I made a quick decision. Round I went, giving each animal an extra pook of hay—a signal which they well understood. Pussy perked up her ears and swished her tail in response. Tedding the wheat straw and placing it beneath their feet, their obvious relief could quite clearly be felt, when they realized they would not have to go out again into the dark, wet field. Instead, they would spend a comfortable night in their warm cowshed. An almost audible sigh of relief passed from cow to cow. Each had the assurance of her own domain: her own drinking bowl and her own personal trough.

How glad we were that we had spent our money building such a comfortable and well-appointed cowshed and dairy. Dudley and I enjoyed a few minutes watching them feed, as they tossed and munched the hay in their mangers. Then we turned off the shed's lights and continued to watch them, silhouetted, through the sliding door. We gently closed all of the doors, put out the dairy lights, and moved swiftly down the track, Adam and Benji close on our heels. The warm van welcomed us all. The dogs were invited in for a quick snack and a warm-up by the fire before being taken back up the hill by Dudley to the office for the night.

Thus began a long autumn and winter routine which took on its daily rituals of cleaning, grooming, milking, and feeding of the stock. It became a set pattern which allowed us more time to move around the farm, make plans for the future, and dream. The pigs were well satisfied in the big sties. The poultry were also content-edly dry and enjoying fresh grass each day, as well as hot mash in the morning and grain at night.

Each day, we watched the falling of the leaves and the chang-ing landscape. Distant views appeared which had been hidden all summer by the dense foliage of the trees. As autumn turned into winter and the temperature dropped, the blue and green of the Graffham downland became a cold slate-grey which gave those gentle hills a gaunt, withdrawn look, as though protecting them-selves against the coming snows of the dank mid-winter. The ponds remained hidden and mysterious in their sheltered hollow. I often went to look for the great golden fish which Noel had placed in one of the small ponds. As I stood silently watching the surface of the water, a ripple came, eventually, and the great golden fish surfaced, glided around for a second, and then disappeared again beneath the cold water. Such a strange, enigmatic creature of the magician's power that seemed to thrive in gentle but alien surroundings, and whose sudden appearance of shimmering gold fascinated me and drew me, time and again, to watch for it in excited anticipation.

One day, when I was down by the ponds, standing completely still by the biggest one, I happened to notice a moorhen darting swiftly across the water to the tiny island in the middle. I saw it on several other occasions, silently darting across the pond, always to the safety of the tiny island, where I was sure that when spring came, she would make a nest to hatch her little brood, safe from foxes and badgers. At its centre, the miniature island had a compact alder bush surrounded by short grass, creating a shelter. The little moorhen had chosen her home so carefully. I hoped that all would go well for them in the springtime. Her secret hideout would remain safe from harm if I, too, kept silent and told only Dudley about it. His protective love of the hidden wildlife was as strong as mine, and as silent.

As the months progressed, the ground became harder and harder with each frost. The water troughs in the fields froze over continuously, needing to be broken free with a crowbar and mallet to allow the water to flow.

In late December, the snow fell silently all night. When we awoke, we found ourselves enfolded in a white wonderland. Since we had kept the coal fire on the entire night, the van was very warm. Dudley, who always had a knack for predicting the weather, was sure, as we closed up the curtains, that snow would come, and it did! Everything was transformed. Our little meadow was white and glistening. I saw a dark streak running alongside the bank. It was the little stream still flowing vigorously, its unknown source moving the water. Even though the water container at the van door was frozen solid, this meant we still had a water supply from the stream for our morning cup of tea.

Dudley got dressed in a warm jumper and thick slacks, pulled on his Wellington boots, and, wrapping himself in his duffle coat, ventured out to get a kettleful of water for our breakfast. It was crisp and dry out, but very cold. I bundled myself up in warm slacks, a woolly jumper, and woollen stockings. The van was so nice and warm, it was difficult to leave its comfort—but the milking *had* to be done.

We trudged up to the yard and entered the cowshed. Eager faces turned as we opened the door. Dudley fetched more hay from the barn while I started to clear back the warm bedding straw from under the cows. The boiler was working, so I soon had a bucket of warm water to wash down the cows' udders. Dudley put the hay around and, whilst they were eating, we prepared the milking units, turned on the engine, and were ready to begin.

By eight o'clock, the milk churns were already on the stand beneath the oak, awaiting the lorry. We then fed the pigs, who cautiously ventured out from their sties, squealing to high heaven as the steaming swill came over the fence straight into their troughs. The noise was quite amazing in this silent, white world.

Having milked the cows and fed the pigs, we felt it was high time to feed ourselves. We let Adam and Benji out of the office, and all together walked back down the slope to the van for a really good, hot breakfast.

Snow in the deep countryside is so dazzling. We kept on looking out of the windows as we ate our breakfast and planned the day's activities. When we had finished, we traipsed up to the yard and out onto the road, where the deep snow had already been swept aside by the snowplough. We reached the top field, fed the hens, and decided against moving the fold units because of the snow. Hot mash, warm water, and the shelter of the nesting boxes was where those tawny birds wanted to be—all huddled together along the perch with their feathers ruffled up against the cold. Later in the day, they would come out and peer at this sparkling white world, *very* suspiciously.

As we stood in the top field and looked across towards Graffham Down, we hardly recognized its familiar contours—so closely wrapped it was in its smooth shroud of pure white. Over at the entrance to the farm, we could still see the great Scots pine, standing out like a beacon, showing the way, just as Dudley had told me in the warm days of summer, when we had first seen the farm. In silent accord, we returned the way we had come, immersed in the pervasive stillness, loath to shatter the spell.

Dudley now had work to do in the office, so after seeing to the rest of the stock, I returned to the van, glad to sit down for half and hour before starting on the rest of my chores. I lay back, savouring the cosy comfort of the bed, and said a big, silent 'thank you' to the Gypsy who had ordered the van, so carefully designed; and to the clever builder in Reading, who had so faithfully manifested his vision. It was truly the most magical home I had ever had, and now I was sharing it with my truelove, as it stood on our own farmland, in this little sheltered meadow with its meandering stream. I thought of our beautiful little Jerseys, warm and comfortable in their new cowshed; the pigs, happy in their deep, straw-littered sties; and the hens, dry, safe, and well-fed in their fold units. Everything seemed to be fine, in spite of the snow, which, in itself, was so beautiful to watch and wonder at.

My reverie was interrupted when Adam jumped up onto the bed and snuggled close to me. How strange this all must be to him, I thought, after the great heat of India, his birthplace! He looked up at me, with a twinkle in his eyes, as if to say, 'It's all right, here close to you.' I pulled the eiderdown over him, and he went to sleep. Everything was so still, so silent, I almost fell asleep myself. Then, I remembered the many things I still had to do: make up the fire, start washing up from breakfast, prepare our dinner, and so on. It all took a long time to accomplish. Reluctantly, I hauled myself off the bed and started.

At midday, Dudley came down to join me in the van. Soon after, Joan Maskelyne came down the track, wearing gumboots and a thick coat, calling out as she walked towards the van, 'Are you all right? You must be terribly cold.' I opened the door and invited her in.

'My goodness!' she said, 'It's so warm and cosy in here, much warmer than *our* house!' We all laughed, and she stayed on until nearly one o'clock, and then went, rather reluctantly, back home to tell Noel how warm *we* were in the van. After we had enjoyed a hot casserole and plum pudding (neither of us feeling the need for conversation), we had another rest until it was time again to resume our usual winter routine.

The snow lasted two weeks, and then slowly dissolved away, leaving the ground and the trees to regain their natural colours and shapes. Life was, indeed, a continual change, and we rejoiced in and with it. Each new day brought us closer together, as we worked side by side, looking after our stock and waiting for the springtime. Each season had its various tasks and joys, which we gladly shared, always making new plans, new ideas, and new suggestions for improvements around the farm. The rhythm of farm life had us completely enthralled now. We experienced that contradictory harmonious feeling of fatigue without much frustration. In the evenings, we read or just talked. It was so satisfying, just being together like this, after so many years of separation. Often, I thought of the gypsy family who had lived in the van, free to come and go as they pleased. We, too, were free to work our own land as we wished, keep stock, and buy and sell, with all the attendant responsibilities and anxieties, as well as unforeseen delights. We were part of the whole. All was progressing as we'd hoped it would.

Christmas in the deep mid-winter came with great excitement, as it does, particularly for children (and we two were children at heart!). We sent greeting cards to all of our friends around the globe and visited the local towns to buy each other special, secret gifts. Then, there was the annual Christmas party and dance at the Graffham village hall (with a surprisingly good band). The whole of Graffham was there, young and old. No one wanted to miss any of the fun. There were balloons and crackers, which created a lot of amusement and laughter. The Maskelynes were there, too, and joined us for the dancing, including Scottish reels and the unusual eightsome reel (for those who knew how it went)—memories, no doubt, from the days of old Laird James Buchanan, a Scot himself, later to become Lord Woolavington. At midnight, we all sang 'Auld Lang Syne,' then started on the homeward journey.

Completely happy on Christmas Day—just the four of us—with our own homespun entertainment, I roasted one of our plump hens and served all the traditional fare: sprouts, carrots, parsnips, roast potatoes, bread sauce and rich gravy, followed by Christmas pudding with brandy butter. That day, Adam and Benji ate until I thought they would burst, and then rushed out of the van to prance and dance it all off. We stayed inside to enjoy coffee and liqueurs. It was a wonderful, leisurely meal for us all.

After the evening milking and the feeding of the stock, we had a light supper. Then Dudley said, 'Let's listen to some music tonight. Would you like that?'

'That would be marvellous,' I exclaimed, 'but how?'

We had no wireless.

With a huge grin, Dudley produced a small portable radio—his Christmas present to the van! He set it on the table and tuned it to Radio 3.

Absorbed in listening to a wonderful concert of music by Ralph Vaughan Williams, we lay together on the bed. The little meadow shimmered as the exquisite sounds filtered out from the van, creating magic on the still night air.

When the music finally ended, I said softly, 'What a *wonderful* conclusion to a perfect day. You really *do* know how to delight my heart, don't you?'

We drew closer, and he whispered, 'This is a time in our life which we will remember always.'

'Oh, yes, always! Working in harmony with Nature, sharing and caring for the land and our animals. This is as it should be, and always will be. A Happy Christmas, darling.'

The End

GREETINGS
from
ADAMS FARM
GRAFFHAM, PETWORTH
SUSSEX

www.ingramcontent.com/pod-product-compliance
Lightning Source LLC
Chambersburg PA
CBHW020811300326
41914CB00075B/1684/J